INSPIRATION,
DECORATION

STARTING POINTS FOR STYLISH ROOMS

INSPIRATION, DECORATION

STARTING POINTS FOR STYLISH ROOMS

JUDITH WILSON

Published by arrangement with
Conran Octopus Limited
Originally published in Great Britain
as *Transforming the Interior*

SIMON & SCHUSTER EDITIONS and
colophon are trademarks of
Simon & Schuster Inc.

Manufactured in China

1 2 3 4 5 6 7 8 9 10

Library of Congress
Cataloging-in-Publication Data
is available.

ISBN 0-684-85680-8

**SIMON &
SCHUSTER
EDITIONS**

SIMON & SCHUSTER EDITIONS
Rockefeller Center
1230 Avenue of the Americas
New York, NY 10020

Contents

INTRODUCTION *6*

COLOR *12*

FABRIC *36*

FURNITURE *60*

POSSESSIONS *76*

NATURAL LIGHT *94*

SPACE *108*

ARCHITECTURAL DETAIL *122*

TRAVEL *142*

LIST OF SUPPLIERS *156*   INDEX *158*   ACKNOWLEDGMENTS *160*

Introduction

Decorating is an emotional issue. Just the thought of it inspires dreams and plans, private passions, the chance to realize new moods, trends, and a fresh way of living. There are luscious colors to try, patterns to explore, shapes, spaces, and light with which to experiment. Nearly all of us embrace the chance to redecorate with enthusiasm and a positive spirit. But the road to redecoration is never an easy one, and even the most strong-minded designer can suffer moments of self-doubt.

Above and Opposite Fresh perspectives. Inspiration for a vibrant decorating scheme comes as readily from a fleeting image as from a color swatch. The fiery red and intense yellow ocher of an Indian sari are interpreted here in bold, dramatic wall colors; and the textile's whorls of pattern are reflected in a curly metal candelabra. Let your starting point lead you to a scheme; then work on creating and refining the finer details.

Standing in a fabric shop, clutching a precious swatch of material, and searching for something to go with it: we have probably all experienced that feeling of panic when faced with the huge choice of patterns and colors available, and the pressure of that revered and dreaded word, taste.

But there is more to redecorating than successfully composing a scheme in this season's colors. Whatever you choose to do in a particular room will become part of your life for the foreseeable future. Every day you will see the new colors, patterns and textures you have selected and, depending on how successful the whole project has been, be inspired, moved, or disappointed by them. What is more, everyone who visits your home will have something to say, a judgment to make, and most of us cannot help but be affected by that as well.

The more you think about it, the more terrifying the whole concept of redecorating becomes. It is little wonder that so many decorating schemes teeter on the brink of something special, even radical, and then fall back into being safe compositions of neutrals, or white with a splash of color. But you do not have to compromise. Putting together a scheme is undeniably a creative process and requires certain skills that can be developed and refined. Some basic guidelines will help to smooth the way from the outset, and these are underpinned by a very simple principle.

Above Use the tones and elements of the landscape. The definite, fresh color seen in this cerulean blue and white sky creates an informal ambience that is further enhanced by casually placed pebbles and striped fabrics.

up at auction, might set you thinking about crisp, tailored slipcovers as well as other upholstery styles that you can mix with them. An influence might be infinitely more oblique—the exotic textures of an embroidered Chinese bag; delicate floral imagery on a perfume bottle label; the mix of gray flannel and red wool spied in a fashion magazine. The possibilities are limitless. The key task is to focus on how and where to seek out your single inspiration and to learn how to interpret it in your decorating scheme.

SOURCES OF INSPIRATION

The most obvious spurs to inspiration are the wider themes we turn to when we decide to decorate—color, pattern, the proportions of a room, and the quality of light. Once you have decided on a particular color or pattern, you have an instant focus. In decorating terms, they are often already captured in a user-friendly form. Fabrics can be touched, and cut straight from the roll; paints can be mixed to order; tiles and trimmings can be bought off the shelf or carefully customized. Key fixed elements such as space and light also need to be considered, planned, and utilized in an essentially practical way. Thus, an abundance of sunshine in the dining room might inspire the use of hot Indian shades such as yellow ocher and tangerine; or a little bedroom may automatically call for a delicate mix of tiny patterns and small-scale furniture.

It is this. Every decorating scheme should evolve from a single point of inspiration, something that so excites and inspires your imagination that you keep coming back to it with a desire to elaborate on it. Everything else—color, texture, pattern—will follow on from this starting point. The focal point that will provide the building blocks for an entire decorating project could come from any one of myriad sources. You might be drawn to an exquisite historic wallpaper in tantalizingly unusual colors, or to a new collection of plain velvets in riotous jewel shades. A curvy little armchair, snapped

To step beyond these conventional, though valid, beginnings, you will need to open your eyes to new influences. This might simply mean walking into the room that is to be transformed and scrutinizing it for precious details—the naturalistic curves of oak leaves fashioned into a central ceiling design, pattern swirled into new plaster, the buttons on the back of a Chesterfield waiting to be re-covered. And become alert to more unexpected sources. Mentally list your most precious possessions. Why do they inspire you? Could the surface design of a cracked but much-loved pitcher inspire a decorating scheme? Are the different shades of color in an artist's postcard the ones with which to transform your bedroom? There might

be a mood you could emulate. Maybe you have felt uplifted by the sculptural use of stainless steel in a restaurant, or by a descriptive passage in a book.

Train yourself to analyze various stimuli in terms of design, color, and contrast. This exercise is not simply about exploring what appeals, but why, and it will also help you to see how separate components work together. Scrutinize shop window displays; examine the way precious objects are laid out in a gallery; notice the subtle, urban tones and textures of a city street and sky. Look, analyze and respond.

FINDING A DIRECTION

Show three individuals the same swatch of patterned fabric and they will each respond

Above Observe chance color combinations. Flashes of hot pink, red, and lime in a Mexican market place inspire colorful upholstery. Such a scene is also recalled in the colors of a rustic kitchen.

Above Building a scheme. The transition from inspirational starting point to finished room relies on first amassing samples. They help you to refine ideas, make choices, and transform them into reality. Include fabric and paint swatches, and samples of door furniture, trimmings, and surfaces. A glass finial may be as significant in the grand scheme as ultra-chic silk stripes.

to it differently. Remember this as you consider your own chosen starting point. The initial attraction of a fabric may be its texture, unusual color nuances, or the evocation of precious memories; but there will be any number of ways of interpreting the fabric in a decorating scheme. It is up to you to seek them out. For example, a piece of 1930s large-scale floral fabric could provide the basis for a whole color scheme that works because the shades already look appealing together on the fabric. But explore other possibilities. Perhaps a bold floral theme could be developed, using a mix of shapes, scales, and colors. Or would the period flavor be more appropriate in your house: say, an authentic 1930s feel in the living room with paint shades and furniture to match? Then again, your fabric may be a temptingly soft, linen weave. Is a textural theme the answer? Keep experimenting until the formula feels right, and always trust your instincts.

CREATING A SCHEME

There are detailed makeovers throughout this book that show a variety of ways in which to put together decorative schemes, but the basics are always the same. Build on your starting point by amassing as many fabric swatches, paint cards, surface samples, flooring ideas, and furniture shapes as you can. Tear out inspirational pictures from magazines, phone or write for catalogs, haunt appropriate shops, and take photographs of furniture and accessories that you like. Dedicate a special area to putting them together, be it a table in the room to be decorated, a scrapbook, or a display board. Then start to experiment with the different elements that you have gathered: try out unexpected color combinations, and lay unusual textures side by side, contrasting scale and seeing what works and what does not. You will need to consider, at all times, the space that you have to decorate, how much natural light there is in a room, the quality of that light, and what architectural features need to be highlighted or hidden. Focus on the furniture you already have, what you need to keep or acquire, and styles for soft furnishings. Decorating is never just about fabrics and colors, but about weaving them around the bare bones of a room to create a composite whole.

FINISHING TOUCHES

When we compose an outfit, we all, consciously or not, add contrasting details, be it a scarlet lipstick with a purple dress, or a jaunty tie with a plain suit. Apply the same idea as you create your living environment.

Any room will be enlivened by little flourishes and highlights, but such details are often neglected in the flurry to finish decorating. You might trace a line of subtle gilding along a molding; add a flash of brightly colored braid to a neutral linen drapery, or display striking sculptural flowers in a contemporary vase. Later chapters have a variety of ideas for detailing, so think about where you might add a vital finishing touch to your decorative scheme.

Left and Below Few of us have the luxury of starting entirely from scratch. Early on, assess the potential of the furniture that is to stay. Can it be revamped with a cool, contemporary textile or regrouped for a fresh silhouette? But be ruthless, too, and decide what can go. Keep only what is essential or what you really love. In this way you enjoy the clearer space or add revitalizingly new pieces.

COLOR

Color surrounds and inspires us. Subconsciously, we register and react to it all the time, but it is easy to take for granted many of the tones seen day to day—the subtle shade of a passing car, the sky at dusk, a pair of theater tickets. Yet colors demand an instant and personal response from every individual. Once a color is introduced onto walls or into furnishings, it automatically becomes a focal point. If we have no experience of putting colors together, we may lack the confidence or may worry about using them, in case they are too bright, do not match, or may slip out of fashion. Yet an interior without color lacks personality, so it is well worth trying to make it work for you.

SOURCES OF INSPIRATION

A single unusual shade, or a clutch of contrasting colors, can make an irresistible and vibrant starting point. If you have pinpointed the exact source of the color—perhaps a paint reference on a chart, or a plain fabric—then you are already a step ahead. It is more likely, however, that you will start by searching for something specific to match an idea of a color in your head, such as "sky blue," or some tones vaguely remembered from another location. In this event, the most practical option is to look through paint charts or swatches of a plain fabric to see and absorb as many varying hues as you can. This can be a fascinating exercise, discovering just how a single color can vary from a muted tone to something clear and bright; how pale it can become; and how dark it can go. Take advantage, too, of being able to put contrasting colors together as you flick through the charts and samples. Often a chance encounter will set off a unique combination that really appeals to you.

Although you will find the biggest range of shades in the major manufacturers' colorcards, seek out specialist paint charts, too. Some of them are individually handpainted instead of printed and, as texture can be integral to the final look of wall colors, this can help enormously. Specialist lines are smaller and you may find them more inspirational because the colors are often temptingly arranged together. For example, a page of blues might vary from chalky pale to rich violet tones, or an unfolding strip may reveal some unusual and delicious neutrals. With fewer samples to choose from, you will certainly focus more quickly on the shade you like. Often their names are so irresistible that they grab your attention and allow you to "see" a color you may otherwise have missed.

Patterned fabrics offer ample inspiration for color, too. The beauty of composing a color scheme using coordinating fabrics is that you can see at a glance that different shades are going to work together, whether they are complementary or contrasting, because the fabric designer has already done the

Above Intense blue walls cheer a plain room, giving a confident contemporary look. A simple, treated wooden table and chairs now seem modern rather than rustic. Distinct pendant lights and monochrome abstract paintings augment the look.

Opposite Hot pink and orange walls become mouthwateringly beautiful when applied in a gentle wash of paint. They make a luscious backdrop to uncompromisingly pretty textiles.

Left The combination of a deep blue sofa and dense dusky pink walls illustrates the essential principle of balancing one strong color with another.

Below Use bright walls to highlight strong shapes. The globe light and monastically styled dining chairs look simply elegant with vivid apple green walls, and a cleverly angled day bed makes an interesting silhouette.

Opposite Play up a bold wall color with a piece of furniture in a similarly strong tone. Dense shades can look fabulously dramatic when teamed with monochrome accessories. The black-and-white wall prints and the aluminum lampshade cut sharply through the cinnamon tones of this modern living space.

thinking. It is also possible to like a color combination and copy it without using the actual fabric. So, even if you want a very plain scheme, it is still worth considering patterned materials and wallpapers as rich initial hunting grounds for color.

Try to absorb as many color influences beyond the confines of traditional decorating media as possible while you are brewing a scheme. The richest pickings will come from the world of fashion. This is not just because the trends in interiors and fashion are becoming increasingly linked, but because influences and colors, textures , and patterns now move so fast in fashion that there will always be a fresh stimulus. Looking at clothes and accessories, and the way they are styled in magazines, is an excellent way of discovering how to use accent colors daringly and successfully. Look also to the natural world, at flowers massed on stalls in the street, seasonal vegetables and their varying hues, the ever-changing tones of the landscape. It requires practice to absorb such influences and to imagine what you see translated onto your walls or floors, but the results can be harmonious, surprisingly racy, and deeply satisfying.

Then there are historical color references. Inspiration may strike when you see a clear and beautiful wall color in an eighteenth-century painting of a rococo interior, or when you visit an historic house. You might spot a soft, authentic shade on a color chart of traditional paints. Do not be constrained and think you can only use historical colors if you are bent on re-creating a particular period feel in a room. Colors transcend centuries, and a Federal green will look just as glamorous in a modern, urban factory conversion as in a carefully preserved historic building.

USING COLOR : THE CHOICES

Say the words using "color" in a decorating context, and some people will assume you mean bright, scary colors like shocking pink or vivid lime. If you do use such colors, you are usually referred to as "very brave." You may need a lot of nerve to opt for bold, clear colours on walls or floors, but the results can be stimulating and refreshing. The benefits of using bright shades are manifold. Singing color is cheerful to live with, and when used on walls provides a wonderful backdrop to show off furniture with unusual lines, or a collection of pictures shouting to take center stage. It can brighten a dull room, distract attention from bumps in plaster, or simply make a fashionable statement if you are well tuned in to current colors. It can lift an ordinary room into the realms of the extraordinary, particularly if used with quirky modern furniture; but, equally, it gives a new slant on a period interior. And it can be used with other surfaces or textures—say, a lime-

colored rubber floor combined with stainless steel, or scarlet wool upholstery with fuchsia pink walls—to provide those essential contrasts that make such interiors so exciting.

The key to using big blocks of bright color is first to keep your nerve, and then to stick unswervingly to the principles of balance and simplicity. Strongly colored walls or floors need at least one other item in the room—an outsize sofa, perhaps, or a bold contemporary rug—that is in an equally heavyweight color to give essential balance. Painting the walls a bright color and hoping that it will jazz up all the other existing mid-toned colors of furniture and accessories simply will not work; they will just look tired and worn. Alternatively, white or neutrals used in great quantity can be excellent balancers for vivid shades. With this look, simplicity in terms of few accessories and uncluttered furniture is essential. If you hesitate at using bright colors on all the walls, consider painting just one, perhaps to highlight a pretty fireplace; or turn the entire concept on its head and go for white walls teamed with definitive pieces of furniture painted or upholstered in the strong colors that appeal to you.

Somber, sophisticated shades, from charcoal to mushroom, plum to sage green, need not be reserved, as some might assume, for historically accurate interiors. Used in the right way, they will look chic and rather worldly, encouraging the fall of natural shadows and contrasts in a room, and promoting a serene ambience. It can take courage to use them, as they are almost as tricky as bright colors to get right. Consider and experiment with them. Their innate subtlety means they can be taken in multiple directions, mixed with pale or rich wood paneling and furniture, mirrors or moldings brushed with silvery tones, and modern metals in any form. Bright colors can work with them fantastically well, too, as part of the main scheme or as an accent shade—think of a clear, orange sofa ranged against an olive green wall or a gray Roman shade trimmed with red linen fringe. Although white looks good

Opposite A subtle scheme using pale, watery mint, lilac, taupe, and white promotes a calm ambience that is ideal in a bedroom. Understated accessories—a chrome shade, a glass full of lavender—reaffirm the style. Decide what mood you want to create before choosing appropriate tones to enhance it.

Above Reassess the power of a deep, somber palette. Used carefully and dressed up with sophisticated styling, it can elevate a room to new heights. The deep gray walls, cream- and biscuit-toned upholstery and dark wood in this dining room succeed because they are teamed up with well-chosen, tailored slipcovers, leopardskin lampshades, and rich pewter.

with somber tones, steer clear of using it conventionally just for the woodwork, as the contrast will be too great. Instead, utilize the tonal shading of colors on paint charts to decide on your deep shade, then choose a pale version of it, or even a different color, for the woodwork. And do not forget texture, as restrained shades can be given extra vitality if they are used on different surfaces.

Using color for contrast, juxtaposition and surprise is one side of the coin. The other relates to light and space. Gravitate toward fresher tones not just because they are "safe" but because they will perform a decorative function for you. Lighter shades, from white through to pale lemon and other pastel tints, may create a tranquil space for working, sleeping, or relaxing, and will open up dark rooms. They are also, quite simply, prettier, if that is a look you want to achieve. But they need to be handled just as skillfully, as too many pale shades together can look dull and insipid. Learn to layer pale colors, using different tones to create a discreet but definite framework to the room. You might use up to five tones of a single color doing this—one for woodwork, another for walls, one for the floor, a fourth for the ceiling, and more for upholstery. It works for colors, and for the whole spectrum of whites, too, which may range from frost to cream. Use this technique in combination with different textures, too, for a harmonious and attractive buildup of visual stimuli.

ACCENTING WITH COLOR

However carefully composed, no color scheme will work properly unless it is accented to some degree with contrast

Above A room devoted to one color gains depth from an interplay of textures. Uneven, painted floorboards, soft bed linen, matte furniture, a translucent window shade, with flowers and the soft outline of a shirt, convert a potentially clinical scheme into a pretty one.

Opposite Variations of tone in related shades give a gentle wash of color. The eau-de-Nil wardrobes, a pastel blue chair, and a spruce green door frame combine to impart a time-evolved air. Consider ways of using different tones together on a wall or on woodwork, instead of just one color on each.

or "detail" shades. The purpose of an accent color is to slightly dislodge equally balanced colors, set things on edge, and make them visually more exciting. Equally, color detailing can be used to draw together apparently disparate hues in a room. It may seem a complex process, but it is something most of us do quite naturally. If you have ever placed a vase of bright green foliage from the garden into, say, a pale blue and white room, you have accented that interior without even realizing it. The vivid color of the foliage serves to crisp up the softer tones in the interior, and encourages the eye to look at the colors in a new context.

Accenting is about surprise and coordination, and it does not have to be a bright color that does the work. In a room full of strong hues, the accent shade might be a neutral or a wood tone; or in an all-white interior, the accent could be a texture—the sheen of an extra glossy white paint, perhaps. And the accent will not necessarily appear as colored upholstery, pillows or trimmings. Notice other details that will work for you. Think of book spines all in one color, mounts in picture frames, the riotous shades of flowers outside the window. You can afford to experiment with accent shades because they are always used in small quantities, so try something even if you think it may not work—and it just might.

TAKING THE PLUNGE

Composing a scheme around color requires precision at the planning stage. If you feel confident using crayons or paints, it can be immensely helpful to draw and color in a rough sketch of how you see the room in your mind's eye. Next, focus on your color samples of paint and fabric. If that elusive shade of paint remains out of your grasp, turn to the specialists. Experts will be able to mix sample colors for you, and certain fabric houses will custom-weave materials or trimmings to order.

When you are amassing swatches, stray a little beyond the colors you have settled on because you might still at this stage make a surprise discovery. If you are collecting pinks, get some scarlet, too. If you are looking for stripes that combine three chosen shades, get one that has a fourth color as well because that might act as your accent color.

Check the contrasts a second and a third time, before applying them to your interior, until you are sure that they are going to work together. Look at them physically in the room, at varying times of the day and if possible during different types of weather, because the play of light will, above all else, determine whether or not your combination of colors will succeed. Too much sunshine, and your sunny turquoise will lose its impact; long afternoon shadows, and that chic gray may seem coldly institutional and depressing.

From the tiny color swatches available it is practically impossible, even for someone with a trained eye, to visualize what a whole room will look like painted a certain color. Get yourself small sample pots, paint large pieces of wall-lining paper or the back of some leftover wallpaper, and pin them up, to give a better idea of the final effect. Live with them for a while; see what a favorite piece of furniture intended for the room looks like

Above Splashes of tangerine, corn yellow, and cranberry in an essentially white space enliven the entire room. Pillows are perfect for color accenting as they are inexpensive and can be changed whenever you are ready for a refreshing new combination.

Right Flowers in punchy colors bring real vitality to a monochrome interior. Searing red gerberas relax the otherwise pristine modernity of this room.

Right Think which surfaces can be used to unbalance a perfectly poised color scheme. A purple painted door juxtaposed with another just glimpsed beyond in cherry red defines and characterizes a modern white interior. Paler accent colors can be equally strong. A run of honey-colored, polished wood set against white walls gives a more subtle contrast.

next to a key color. Remember, bright colors will drain paler shades, and the intensity of all-over wall color can even throw a sickly cast over paler tones. Equally, what looks like a definite ice-cream shade on a paint chart, may be swallowed up in a big room and look more like a dull white. You may need to go up a shade to achieve the correct depth of color. If you have chosen a bright color as the key to your scheme, and intend to use it for curtains or shades, drape a sample over the sofa or at the window. What looks like electric blue on a sampleboard may pale to insignificance when suffused with natural light. You may need to line draperies to retain the essence of the color, or choose another medium for including that blue in your scheme. Remember, the color of your draperies, especially their lining, will affect the exterior appearance of your house.

You may think scale is more relevant to pattern than to color, but considering how much of a color to use is absolutely vital. Looking at three identically sized swatches of your chosen key colors will give a false impression. Try to gauge the balance of color by cutting down your samples in proportion to how each will be used—a big piece of the color intended for a capacious wing chair, say, and relatively smaller pieces to represent pillows. And remember that in a scheme based purely on plain colors, you can be really adventurous with different textures. Start with textiles, and go on from there, drawing in the smoothness of colored plastics, the translucence of glass, the pleasing irregularity of handmade tiles, or the bite of a raised rubber floor.

The Acid Test

A chance combination of wild and subtle shades can inspire a decorative idea in the same way as a single strong color. This stack of brightly colored ceramics in crushed plum, grass green, and acid sherbet yellow provides the stimulus for a dynamic and experimental color scheme in a small studio apartment. Their fresh, modern tones open out the space and give this period environment a new, contemporary feel.

Above Keep a watchful eye in stores for color inspiration: piles of merchandise like these ceramics in colliding colors may form the nucleus of a novel palette.

Right Despite its subdued grays and drab drapes, it is obvious that this gracefully proportioned room has plenty of potential.

Opposite Dashing, confident color and a touch of irreverence can twist the period detailing of a room, creating a fresh, contemporary environment.

Slick, fashionable shades are tempting to use. For a season or two they are everywhere, and sensitize the eyes to colors that are addictively vivid but which can be difficult to live with. Using these colors in such a graceful room needs thought. With its elaborate coves, dramatic floor-to-ceiling windows, and,

attractive wrought-iron balconies, not all "modern" color combinations will be successful. Due consideration should be given to a contemporary color scheme like this—the combination of acid yellow and plum—to insure that the attraction will not fade when next season's palette comes around.

Double doors lead straight from the living room into a hi-tech, stainless-steel kitchen in this apartment. The owner's tastes veer toward minimal styling and a contemporary mood, so a vivid color scheme is ideal. Using a trendy sherbet yellow on the walls means that in years to come the color can easily be whitewashed out in favor of subtler tones. The more definite shades like deep plum can be kept for upholstery.

Finding the middle ground

With sharp sherbet yellow walls it is important to use the right color for the ceiling and the woodwork. Brilliant white is not always the answer as it can look too new and may reduce the depth of color on the walls. In this room, it would also make the pale marble fireplace look dirty. Instead, a subtle lavender gray defines the woodwork; although this looks quite dark on the paint card, once painted it blends comfortably with white. The color of the floor is also important. Boldly painted walls need either another strong, clear color to balance them—perhaps as painted boards, or vivid linoleum—or the right neutral. Here, a green-tinged seagrass matting has been chosen to cover the floorboards because it complements the acid color of the walls.

After the background "canvas" is complete, decorator fabrics need to be chosen. These are used to introduce the plums and grass green, possibly more acid yellow, and, inspired by the woodwork, tones of lavender and mauve. In a scheme dominated by such strong colors, textures will need to work harder if they are to be noticed. The hard-edged stainless steel in the kitchen prompts the use of shiny taffetas and silks; these fabrics, traditionally the reserve of elegant

Opposite The naturally intense colors of a bunch of flowers are often all that is needed to enliven a carefully coordinated scheme. The amethyst tints and vibrant greens of these scabious do not exactly match the plums and greens in the room, but are sharper versions of the same shades.

Above Clip swatches into a sketchbook, along with snapshots of pieces of furniture in need of a revamp.

Left Play with accent colors even after a room is complete. This pale turquoise cup, introduced by chance, looks absolutely right against the silver and citrus background.

upholstered in a fashion-conscious new fabric and teamed casually with a coffee table on wheels. Giving a new twist to period interiors does not simply mean exuberantly colored walls; it also depends on how you deal with received images of classic furniture shapes.

Window dressing

Devising successful window treatments in a room awash with brilliantly colored walls is more complex. Unless the fabric is similarly bold or deliberately neutral, it may dilute the impact of both colors. If the emphasis is firmly on a slick, modern finish, as it is in this room, curtains can be ruled out; shades will also show off the beautiful windows. As soon as the old drapes were removed from the windows, the room seemed to open out and breathe again. Vivid lime-checked roll-up shades fit discreetly into each recess and are all that is needed; at night, the working shutters can be drawn across for privacy.

Metallic highlights

Walls and furnishings in vivid colors are exhilarating, but if strong color is used everywhere in a room it can become exhausting. Neutrals will cool everything down, and so too will metallics. Think of them as an extra shade in the color spectrum. Here, the cue is taken from the stainless-steel kitchen, and silvery metals in modern shapes are introduced to build on the contemporary angle. A brushed aluminum mirror frame, a silvery pendant light, and a punched-steel dining chair, and beaten pewter bowls all set the right upbeat tone, while the cool color and smooth texture of the marble coffee table and fireplace tie in with these metallic highlights.

Some paint colors look so glorious on walls that it is tempting to leave them totally unadorned. However, in this studio apartment, simply framed black-and-white art photographs look chic and understated. If anything, a citrus yellow gives them greater impact than a brilliant white.

living rooms, are used here as chic square pillows. To add a softer dimension to this contemporary scheme, classic textures are chosen for the upholstery: striped chenille for the sofa, and chartreuse- and grape-colored linen to unify two wildly different styles of armchairs.

Once it is set against vivid walls, the furniture is thrown into sharp relief. A 1950s-inspired armchair with splayed legs is deliberately picked for its glorious silhouette, as is a modern floor lamp with a crisp, pleated shade. The traditional three-seat sofa looks good in this modern milieu because, instead of being swamped in a conventional cover, it is tightly

Opposite However dense and bright fabric shades seem, look at them in direct sunlight to see what happens. A grape-colored linen armchair is so saturated with color that it holds its own against the sherbet-colored walls.

Above A dash of warm, rich red in a cluster of anemones offers a stimulating highlight amid the prevailing cooler tones.

Right If you dare, pick one shade brighter than your initial choice for windows, because sunlight will dilute its impact. And make what goes into your window box an integral part of the scheme; here, red geraniums give a definite edge to the apple green voile shade.

Natural Neutrals

The softest and subtlest neutral hues take their cue from the natural world: a pile of field-fresh mushrooms, sea-washed stones, or lichen-covered bark all provide inspiration. When examined, each can be seen to contain its own perfect and complete palette of bleached shades, from cream to oyster, and from sage to ash. The warmth and depth of nature's tones can be used to smooth a kitchen's modern lines and generate a peaceful, welcoming ambience.

The ideal family kitchen should act as the cohesive center of the home, reconciling its different functions with its overall look. It should be sleek and efficient, but it should also be user-friendly for children and easy to transform for grown-up dinner parties. This kitchen has great potential because it is large, long, and sunny. A warm creamy-toned scheme is instantly on the agenda because it will blend easily with the newly laid white-oak floor and the original bleached-pine hutch and built-in cabinet. The appeal of such a scheme lies in its comfort value. Even if you desire state-of-the-art efficiency, this look will take the scary edge off modernity.

A kitchen should be planned to transcend the vagaries of fashion, so that a decade on, there is no sinking feeling that it is wildly out of step with current style. Classic, natural textures, a soothing, "barely there" color scheme, and pared-down detailing, provide the perfect solution.

Above Give more than a cursory glance to fruits and vegetables. Learn color lessons from their variegated tones, which sweep from light to dark.

Left A large room needs boundaries. Decide at the start on spaces for eating, relaxing, and cooking, and balance function with the final aesthetic vision.

Opposite A blend of cream and honey tones combines with frosty pastels to create a welcoming family kitchen.

Natural surfaces

A kitchen's surfaces are all-important. The narrow run of a countertop, the massed cabinets, and the tiling all need to tie in with your chosen colors. Cream paint for cabinets and walls blends well with the fudge tones of the floor. To complement the shiny stainless steel, a charcoal-veined marble as countertop and backsplash makes a classic addition. To continue the neutral theme, chrome outlets, opaque glass lampshades, and roll-up shades of white punched cotton are chosen. This is not a style that needs any fussy fabrics.

Kitchens need plenty of storage space for good organization and control. This is one room in the house where there is a constant influx of objects that will interfere with a pared-down vision. This kitchen has enough cabinets to keep less attractive items at bay, leaving the hutch as a focal point for displaying the unpretentious ceramics and garden flowers that work with, not against, the total scheme. More importantly, good storage means that worktops are freed up and can be used to keep practical accessories at hand—Mediterranean-style white platters, a marble pestle and mortar, and chrome appliances.

Above Functionality and style converge: ultra-smooth marble, vanilla paint, the palest oakwood flooring, and pristine punched cotton combine to provide flawless but practical surfaces. Create a working colorboard with hard surface samples, drawing in contemporary silvery accents with essentials like outlets and shade pulls.

Left Match glasses, utensils, and ceramics to the overall vision. The enduring simplicity of chunky glasses takes its cue from the unadorned cabinets and scrubbed wooden table.

Opposite Continental chic meets simple country: a shock mixture of styles allows for a family dining space with many faces. With white platters, plain glasses, and casual raffia mats, the chunky wooden table creates a no-nonsense breakfast style.

Opposite Ice-cream-colored chairs, the rosy blush of hydrangeas, formal napkins, and minimalist place settings create, in minutes, an elegant dinner party mood in the heart of the kitchen.

Right A sliver of windowsill, a mantelpiece, or the top of a kitchen cabinet, each possesses display potential combined with practical appeal. Unassuming china, cunningly aligned and spiced up with a single flower, transforms itself into an engaging still-life.

Below Original period features—a fireplace, a cupboard—are seamlessly drawn into the contemporary scheme, by dint of modern styling and a light touch with accessories. A regimented row of wonderfully shaped pots looks fresh and new, while crisp, linen-covered pillows add a touch of unfussy comfort.

Ice-cream colors

The danger of having a cream kitchen is that it can easily take on a country aspect. Where urban elegance is required, as here, replace too much pine with continental-style chairs in the palest ice-cream colors—frosty blue, pistachio, and lemon. These colors have nothing to do with baby blue and sugar pink, and everything to do with new-age style and modern plastics. The two contrasting palettes create a sophisticated edge. In addition, napkins and ceramics in ice-cream shades serve to conjure up a smarter ambience for casual dinner parties.

Spicy accents

A kitchen needs to allow for changes of mood between one area and another. Efficient stainless steel can predominate at the cooking end, while frosty pastels feature in the dining space. A leather armchair or wicker baskets and pots in nuttier browns can change the pace again, taking the cream and honey tones into a more relaxed vein.

FABRIC

Fabrics contain numerous elements that can elicit a personal response— the feel, fall, color shades, texture, pattern, and design. Furnishing fabrics influence the very mood of a room, indicating sophistication or simplicity, reflecting modern trends, or providing historical authenticity. Equally, a swirl of fabric introduced into a room can, chameleon-like, change its own look to attune to its surroundings.

The fabrics you choose signify your taste and personality for all the world to see, but they are also supremely functional. As a medium that is available in so many forms, fabric offers literally hundreds of choices. And in decorating terms, the selection of one design is not an end but a beginning because it is a rare fabric that is used alone.

of styles and colors. A surprise find may turn your ideas around and make for a fresher, and more uniquely personal result. Fabric retailers invariably push their latest collection, but explore their earlier collections as well. Consider the way fabrics are put together in retailers' sample books. The age of the totally coordinated room has gone but most companies include solid-colored fabrics, small-scale weaves or prints, and wallpapers in matching tones to help you choose. To glean other soft furnishing inspiration, look at how fabrics are styled in advertisements or catalogs.

Exploring alternative sources can be satisfying. They may turn up a unique fabric pattern, and using a fabric unconventionally will make it especially interesting in an interior. Track down theatrical suppliers for different weights of burlap, unbleached muslin, or canvas. Scour dress fabric departments for unusual cloths. Think laterally about other fabric uses. What about wools and shirtings, or catering mail-order firms that sell linen dish towel fabric, striped roller towels, and large tablecloths? Search out specialist mail-order fabric companies that deal just with silks, say, in every conceivable weight and color. A card crammed with swatches might spark ideas for color or textural combinations.

Losing preconceptions about decorator fabric and looking at textiles from other contexts is essential. See what other departments in your local store have to offer. Consider if a white drawn-threadwork sheet might look good as a curtain or whether a silk scarf in outrageous colors would look fantastic on the seat-pad of a chair. Look afresh at the clothes shelves. A shift in fashion toward slippery, satin textures might suggest a boudoir feel for a bedroom; or the sight of piles of denim jeans might set you off on the trail of colored denims.

A specific piece of fabric that has inspired you may not be available in quantity, but a frayed square of novelty cotton may set off a character-inspired mural in your child's bedroom. You might have a length of handprinted silk in irresistible colors,

SOURCES OF INSPIRATION

Fabrics offer enormous scope for experimentation. The multi-colored or patterned features of material provide instant inspiration. Whether it is crisp, unfussy blue-and-white stripes or the watercolor shades and country mood of a finely drawn English rose print, such defining characteristics should set you on a fail-safe path toward a working decorative scheme.

The most obvious inspirations will come from decorator fabrics themselves, ranging from the latest retail collections to those from more specialist trade suppliers, whose materials will only be available through interior design shops or the designers themselves. You may already have a theme or color in mind when you start looking but keep an open mind and look at lots

Opposite A single motif unifies a scheme. The combination of checks in varying scales gives an informal air. Beyond upholstery exploit the potential of tablecloths, napkins, or a throw to strengthen themes.

Right A fail-safe combination of florals and stripes is linked by delicate tones of lichen and cherry. Ticking stripes next to overblown roses, and crisp Oxford borders next to frilly ones create charming contrasts.

Above Sometimes, a bold fabric design is all that is needed to pull together a crisp and punchy look. The white-and-cream linen stripes on the draperies, shade, and outsize pillows are allowed to dominate this sophisticated living room, while their surroundings are deliberately kept subdued and neutral. Blue delphiniums and a zany zebra rug make brilliant finishing touches.

Above A combination of similarly scaled but unrelated patterns creates an informal interior. The lime, aqua, and cherry tones in the painterly stripes and madras check provide color links. Using scale and color like this results in a sun-filled kitchen that has a contemporary, just-put-together feel.

Opposite This vast and wacky living room, with its wild mix of patterns and color, works because underlying its mad palette of tangerine, gray, sherbet yellow, and aqua is a commitment to detail. Broadly striped pillows tie in with a freestanding screen, while the batik print is counterbalanced by the huge geometric shapes in the rug on the floor, which in turn are echoed in the abstract painting above.

bought direct from a textile-design student. Whether it is a remnant, a sale bargain, or your grandmother's old curtains, you must love it enough for the scheme built around it to endure for a number of years.

FINDING A DIRECTION

At the outset, focus on the physical characteristics of fabric and the interpretations they suggest. Most of us are attracted to patterns because they offer instant visual stimulation. Consider not only other patterns and scales of patterns with which they could be mixed, but also what color combinations are possible. Is there textural detailing that can be exploited? Is the feel of the material or the way it gathers in your hand important, or does it suggests a certain curtain treatment? Practicality with a touch of frivolity also counts. If you have a young family, it would be wise to pass up silk brocade for the sofa and go for hard-wearing textiles, but a dry-cleanable pillow covered in a sumptuous fabric could add a touch of adult sophistication.

Be on the lookout for fabrics that can be customized. Tea staining and washing will impart a gentle shabbiness to plain cottons, but always do it before stitching, in case the dyeing does not produce the effect you want. Embroider a motif or monogram, appliqué if you have the patience, or trim a curtain or pillow with beading. Insetting a panel of fabric into a contrasting one, pintucking, patchworking large squares of plain fabrics, and appliqué are all ways to create more exciting textiles than may otherwise be available.

CONSIDERING SOFT FURNISHINGS

Fabrics for decorating schemes cannot be looked at in isolation; you must think specifically about their use in soft furnishing terms. The fabric itself may dictate its most flattering incarnation. For example, a large-scale pictorial cloth would look better used in a Roman shade than lost within the folds of draperies. Or you might need a specific type of material to realize an idea. And many designs, such as paisley, would look equally good in a variety of forms.

For window treatments, consider not only whether a fabric will become draperies, a roll-up or Roman shade, or unlined panels, but also if a grand or simple style is appropriate, what kind of heading you want, whether to use metal or chunky wood poles, a shaped valance, or a lambre-quin. Much of these considerations will derive from the fabric you choose, but consider, too, the context of the architectural style of a room, the total look you want to achieve and what furniture you have. What about trimmings, customized detailing, contrasting linings or edgings, voiles, or a separate sun shade?

Whether you are looking at fitted upholstery or slipcovers, the fabric is crucial. As well as the style, you will need to consider practicalities such as whether your fabrics are designed for heavy upholstery use and whether they can be washed. Deciding about upholstery always seems scarier than dealing with window treatments, but it offers a lot of scope for individual and creative detailing, and inventive upholstery often grabs more attention than draperies, which may have to compete with a great view. Think about different furniture styles. Do you want upholstered furniture or loose slipcovers for a more relaxed feel? Will the dining chairs be upholstered in different colors for variety, perhaps with contrasting fabrics on the back and the seat, or will you perhaps want to concentrate on the details? Think about matching or contrasting welting, button, tie, or pocket details, or just re-covering the seat-pad of a cozy armchair in a different fabric. Thinking up unusual solutions makes the process fun, not

overwhelming. Extend that frivolity to fabric detailing, too. Pillows, bed-covers, throws, tablecloths, and lampshades all have potential for enriching a scheme.

USING FABRIC: THE CHOICES

Selecting your ideal fabric is one thing. Deciding how to balance it with existing features and other component fabrics in the room is more complex. You will have to make choices about mixing patterns, especially in relation to scale, balance, and color; coordinating themes; and building up textures. There may be a clue in your fabric that helps. A floral pattern motif with a background stripe is asking for a relaxed mix of the two elements, but it is not always that simple.

Opposite A fabric with an ornate design executed on a grand scale deserves to be seen flat. Textiles stretched onto a frame on a wall give a sophisticated, rich effect that can be expanded by use on a headboard or chair.

Right The restrained, neutral palette of this bedroom looks extra chic with its crisply tailored plain fabrics and their contrasting borders.

Far Right Drawn-threadwork linens, smooth wool, nubby herringbone, and other textured fabrics could be the starting point of a country theme.

Big, bold patterns, often first to catch our attention, are frequently wasted. Once we have daringly made the selection for, say, draperies, most of us fight shy of repeating it, in case the effect becomes overpowering. But it is a mistake to abandon a statement pattern without a visual reminder of it elsewhere. Even scattering related pillows on it will help anchor it into the overall scheme. Let your bold design enjoy center stage. Use it right across your upholstered furniture and at the windows for a unifying effect, especially when walls and floors are kept plain. If you want to reduce the impact of the scale slightly, add something surprisingly outsize, a checkerboard floor, perhaps. Or mix it with several other large-scale but slightly different patterns—this works excellently with stripes or checks—to provide balance and some extra contrast.

If your fabric pattern is large-scale but not too dominant, for example a toile de Jouy, you can mix it with plain fabrics to keep attention firmly focused on the design; or you could add

interest and depth by teaming it with smaller-scale, companion patterns. There are certain classic combinations that always work—toile de Jouy and checks, florals with stripes—but find your own versions, too. There are few rules for this kind of mixing, although using only one or two unifying colors helps. Experimenting with varying scales is the key. Or simply forget about companion patterns, and team your pictorial design with matching, same-scale wallpaper. If such a thing does not exist, use the fabric stretched over the walls, too. It is a braver choice and looks assured and confident.

Consider thematic links where related motifs unify a number of patterns. Such a link can be very obvious, with a large-scale botanical print used alongside smaller leaf-design companion fabrics and antique botanical engravings on the walls. Or the visual references may be more subtle. A combination of fabrics sporting circle motifs with round tables, circular detailing on a chair, and a round mirror could draw

Left Plain fabrics are easily customized. Translucent, unlined cotton panels, silk-screened with a giant red rose, contrive to look both contemporary and yet pretty in a casual living room.

Opposite Explore the movement, touch, and look of fabric for its innate mood. Dense, rich, rust-colored velvet contributes to the romantic atmosphere in a room with ocher paint-washed walls and candle-effect lighting. Heavy damask pillows and draperies reinforce the mood.

the whole room into the scheme. Simpler versions might include mixing a number of florals, stripes, or checks to create a casual, relaxed look. Color and scale may be less important when there is a strong unifying motif.

Pattern does not inspire everyone and a plain scheme that relies on texture can be very chic. The textural characteristics of fabrics with their own very subtle patterns are another rich vein of inspiration. Imagine a graphic jumbo cord, plain fabrics with a subtle stripe in the weave, or a pintucked silk; the complex patterns created by a mixture of herringbones of different scales; or bobbly sisal flooring combined with the raised texture of tapestry and the regular, nubby texture of a rib-knit pillow. Then focus beyond fabrics to add other, less obvious patterns: stripes of light coming through a Venetian blind to go with the jumbo cord, say; or the latticed cane of a Bergère

chair to emphasize the close-woven pattern of an Indian gauze. Including flooring here is crucial because carpet, woven fibers and wood create their own very definite patterns. Texture has a sensual quality, too. An entire scheme could be woven around feel-good materials: the soft touch of velvet, fake fur, suede, even terry cloth. Add throws that can be cuddled up to, a footstool to caress bare feet, and soft wool draperies that are both fluid and tactile.

ACCENTING WITH FABRIC

However much attention you have paid to balancing and contrasting color in a heavily fabric-focused scheme, think afresh about accenting. An unexpected flash of colored fabric is a key option. Your soft furnishing details, such as a contrasting lining or buttoning on a chair, could provide it. But contrasting patterns or textures make serious statements as well. You can add real verve to a room by introducing a different scale, perhaps with an extravagantly outsize print on one pillow cover; or uplift a restrained combination of matte textures with a dining chair covered in glitzy Chinese embroidery. Accenting can affect the mood of a room. A stark modern interior using crisp new fabrics can be saved from looking clinical by the apparently casual addition of a couple of antique throws.

MAKING IT HAPPEN

The difference in appearance between a small swatch of fabric and two yards (or meters) showing the whole pattern repeat is terrifying. Take home as long a length of fabric as possible; most shops have returnable samples. Live with your fabric in the room you will be decorating. Scrunch it up at the window, spread it over sofas, tuck it around pillows. Check how it looks in the light and in relation to the architectural character of the room and the floor texture. A simple checked cotton looks great with floorboards, but may be less appropriate with carpet. Is the fabric at odds with your existing furniture or will it provide an interesting contrast?

With a large-scale design, a small swatch of fabric is misleading because you cannot see how the pattern works as a whole. You might focus on a single rose in it, only to find that on a larger piece of the cloth the same rose pales into insignificance among a trailing trellis of ribbons. What seems to be a gently rambling pattern repeat may become unsuitably geometric when seen over a large area. If you focus specifically on a tiny motif on a swatch of a fabric with a small-scale design, you may not realize until too late that, spread over a large area such as a headboard, the pattern becomes a blur of dots, with crucial colors lost in an unplanned sludge. Also, the play of light can alter the appearance of plain and textured fabrics by diminishing the intensity of the color; or, from certain angles, failing to highlight an interesting weave pattern.

After considering all your curtain or soft furnishing options, it will be time to make specific decisions. Cultivate a flexible curtain maker and/or upholsterer. Make your own sketches, however rudimentary, of ideas you want to try. A professional will be able to interpret a look in practical terms from your pictures or drawings.

It will not be until you have an estimate of how much fabric is needed that you will know how expensive your scheme is going to be. Sometimes, the need to cut down on quantity generates a more inspired result. Your favorite fabric may have to be used only as a broad border on a curtain made of a cheaper plain fabric; or your armchair be made up in burlap instead of linen. Such compromises often look more individual. And there is nothing as satisfying as knowing that you have spent less and still achieved ravishing results.

Classic Pattern

A classic toile de Jouy evokes the elegance and style of a grand French château. Pictorial and ornate, it demands to be taken seriously, yet its subtle shades inspire prettiness, too. This one, in faded deep purple and parchment, forms the backbone of a large room that combines both living and dining areas. Confidently mixed with smart stripes and opulent textures, this toile de Jouy imparts freshness with a touch of grandeur.

It is hard to fail with a classic fabric design, a toile, or possibly a floral chintz. Invariably beautifully colored, with a timeless appeal, they are unlikely to fall out of favor because they transcend fashion. Yet you cannot ignore the sometimes rigid style associations that such a classic brings with it. Of course toile de Jouy has the air of a French château, a hint of period living. It is the degree to which you interpret those connotations that will dictate if a scheme is new and original or a mere copy of what has gone before.

This living room benefits from plenty of light and suitably grand proportions. As it serves as both a living room and a dining room, the fabrics chosen need to mark out changes in the key areas, while the palette remains tonally strict. A toile offers the scope to do both. It mixes quite easily with stripes, plain fabrics, and other toiles, and its characteristic dual tones keep color choices relatively simple.

Above With its purple and dipped-tea tints, a classic toile sets an entire room scheme in motion.

Left This Victorian room has plenty of light and good proportions, qualities that have been exploited in this fresh, cool scheme.

Opposite The power of a classic design: from a single toile comes a dining room suffused with the romantic air of a French château. Crisp tailoring, distressed furniture, and detailed flourishes complete the transformation.

Left The success of a living room lies not just in its surface detail, but in the way furniture is arranged to promote comfort and ambience. Place seating in intimate groups so that you do not have to shout across the room, and keep side tables realistically close so there is always somewhere to put down a drink.

Opposite, above Look out for antique fabrics in specialist shops, sales, and markets. A piece of furniture covered in something authentic can be intellectually, as well as decoratively, satisfying.

Opposite, below Using ornate fabrics like silks and satins may seem difficult, not only because they are more expensive but also because you may not want too formal a look. The key is to supplement your favorites with simpler linens and cottons, and choose wonderful colors that pull together the whole look. The warm deep purple in the toile is repeated throughout the scheme, shifting tonally to plum and purple, and then to paler silvery mauve.

A luxurious touch

You can be very grand with toile, or monastically simple. This room finds a midway path by interpreting the ornate French château style with rich, decadent fabrics and by restricting the use of toile to chic little slipcovers in the dining area alone. Too much toile can easily look fussy, and this room needs to be grown-up without being too stiff. The luxury element comes from the texture of the fabrics, rather than their patterns. A sofa becomes invitingly sophisticated covered in a sensual velvet, as does a Victorian chaise longue dressed in an antique satin. Continuing the theme, a modern satin stripe is used on the chair.

These are all formal fabrics and yet they sit happily in this room because they are used simply. Getting it right is vital. Silks and satins frequently feel overpowering because they have been trimmed with grandiose fringing, or because they have

been used in abundant swathes. Here, however, the chairs have self-welting with no extraneous detailing. At the windows, where silk draperies might have swung the balance of style, there is only white cotton lace. This performs a dual function. Not only does it tone down unnecessary grandness, but it allows maximum light into the room.

Carefully matching fabric patterns impart formality, but a more relaxed mix is much easier to live with. Thus, a patterned stripe and a simple stripe, with a plain velvet and an expanse of white linen tablecloth, move the toile a step away from its grandiose feel toward a more original combination, with a touch of modernity. Freshness comes, too, from plain walls in a mixture of cool gray and white, and from floorboards that are sanded and washed down with white latex.

Shades of color, all variations on the two-tone toile, are necessary for uniting this dual-purpose room. To play on the parchment hues would create too antique a feel; instead a shift from cream to palest gray lightens up the whole palette.

Opposite Where a single long room has a contrasting function at each end, pay attention to how you divide the two areas both physically and visually. A stately chair in the French style bridges the gap between formal dining area and the prettier sitting area, and its cream-and-plum stripe draws together the varying strands of color.

Below A lean and romantically curved glass jar, crushed-purple pleated ribbon, and a crystal salt dish combine on a stiff white cloth. The contrast of decadence and simplicity gives the dining table a decorative edge.

Above The gentle scrolls on the toile find their match on a mantelpiece. Pretty moldings should be echoed by accessories like decorative painted porcelain.

imparts a time-worn air and looks at ease with toile. A tumbling glass chandelier, though not of the correct period, gives the feel of a château. Think about what accessories can do to heighten the mood. While the dining area is formal, this living room aims for a tranquil and relaxing ambience. The portrait of a woman, a floral oil in minty green and pink, scrolled teacups on the mantelpiece, all create an elegant and intimate atmosphere.

On the dining table, essential components of glassware, china, and silverware echo the themes of the room in another way. New biscuit-toned floral china cuts through the starchy whiteness of an antique cloth, and simply blown wine glasses contrast with a decorative swathe of pleated plum ribbon. On the table, meanwhile, the colorful potential of fruit and food has been exploited to the full. Vivid purple grapes and dark red wine bring the coolness of the dining area utterly to life.

The deep purple provides the starting point for the other fabrics. Reinterpreted as silvery mauve in the velvet and patterned stripe, and sharpened to plum in the satin stripe, these tones are given an edge when accented with blood-red tulips.

Fine-tuning the room

Interpret one vein from a particular style, and it will follow a trajectory of its own. The grandness of toile cries out to be paired with French furniture, so cane and wooden chairs, a distressed mirror, and an occasional table with a touch of gilding form the core of this room's furniture. But it is so much more a case of borrowing from the look, rather than adapting it wholesale. And you can cheat. A new gilded Louis XIV chair can be made to look aged or, washed in the palest gray, even the most unremarkable mirror frame can be cleverly disguised.

So, in a room that takes at least some of its inspiration from a fabric classic, look to accessories to weave in period elements. Petit-point needlework, on a pillow and a rug,

Cozy Textures

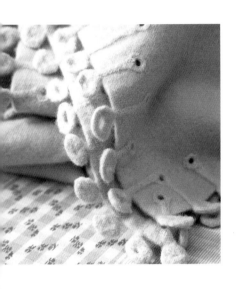

The allure of a special fabric lies as much within its weave as in the pattern. A glassy starched linen, crumply waffle cotton, or tough mattress ticking all provide unique beginnings for reinventing a room. The wintry soft wool and ice-blue shading of this throw prompt new ideas about how to decorate a shadowy, low-ceilinged country guest room. Key elements in this scheme are the interplay of a cool color palette and generous textures.

Above Thick and tactile textiles drape well. Consider them not just for a comforting throw, but as dramatic curtains or a luxurious covering for a fireside armchair.

Right This charming cottage bedroom features sloping floorboards polished over centuries, a deep window seat, and a low, beamed ceiling.

Opposite The room's principal disadvantage is a lack of sunlight, so the terra-cotta walls are replaced by planes of cool, light color.

It is a huge leap from choosing a throw to creating an entire sampleboard ready for action. Analyzing a room will provide invaluable decorative guidance. As this is a characterful bedroom, with chunky polished old floor-boards and bowing walls, mixing the smooth wool throw with cozier country textures will create the right feel. A deeply recessed window means that the bedroom is quite dark. So, although walls painted pale blue-gray will maximize the sunlight, the scheme will also need warming tones to bring it to life. Glancing out of the window on a winter's day finalizes the palette. Red rose-hips, hoar frost, and a pale gray winter sky look so glorious outside, it is almost certain they will work within.

Celebrating a country cottage room with classic, rustic motifs and artisan-style furniture seems entirely appropriate. The pastoral scenes on a French toile, teamed with gingham, produce the perfect, timeless mix.

MIRABELLE

A soft touch

A bedroom is the one room filled with textiles that do not come off the roll. Sheets, blankets, quilts, throws, and pillowcases can be individual handworked pieces and will all contribute their own textures. The scheme in this room is to be done in reverse, starting with the bed. This is appropriate here as the bed is the focus of the room. Curtains come later; the initial search is for soft country weaves. Comforting waffle blankets, a cherry-colored quilt, sheets in crisp cotton and heavy neutral linen, and finally a rich red plaid throw, all add complementary textures. The crowning glory is a pair of puffy feather quilts, made up in the red-and-white gingham that is central to the scheme.

To give full rein to the glorious mix of textures on the beds, the rest of the room is a simple canvas worked out in three colors: a cherry-red toile de Jouy to match the gingham, heavily woven white linen and canvas, and an ice-blue stripe and check to reinforce the initial color reference. The pictorial toile would have looked too grand as curtains, so instead it is used in a broad strip on thick country drapes. White canvas for the window-seat cushion reflects as much light as possible, while cushion covers and a chair seat are made up from pale blue fabric.

The walls are washed in sky-blue tones, a paint shade carefully picked from an historical range so that it is in keeping with the period nature of the room. The furniture, deliberately chosen last, is unadorned and rustic, and has been simply painted with a pure white latex to tie it in with the overall scheme. Similar pieces can be found at country fairs.

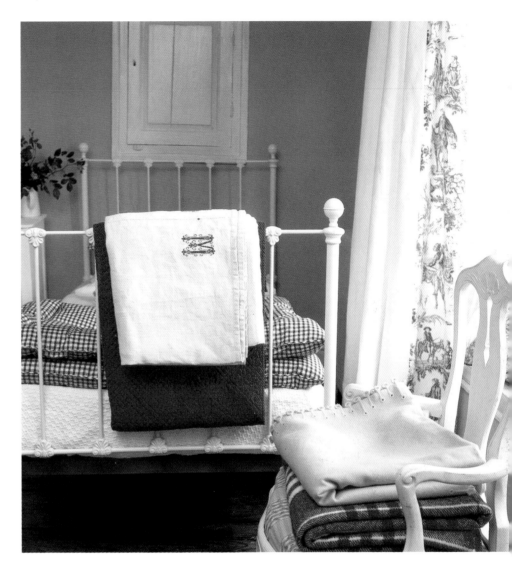

Opposite A riot of patterns—gingham with toile, stripes with sprigs—takes on a cohesive look if married together within the confines of a strict two- or three-color palette. For an under-stated scheme like this, it is essential to mix plain fabrics with patterned ones. Keep to a unifying background color to hold everything together: fresh white is the key in this collection.

Above Thoughtful detailing counts in a guest bedroom. A side chair on which to fold clothes, extra blankets in case of cold, crisp cotton sheets, and a vase of fresh garden flowers will all make overnight visitors feel extra welcome.

Graphic Motifs

A rose, a bee, a twirling leaf: for every random pattern, there is another featuring the simple repetition of bold, parallel lines. These fabrics are rarely the central players in a scheme: rather, they are for mixing and layering, for the fleshing out of themes and the bolstering of grand designs. Yet this beautiful figured Spanish embroidery contains the kernel of an idea for the dramatic transformation of a light-filled city apartment.

This second-floor living room is broad and sunny with—unusually for a city apartment—two sets of French doors. The apartment had not been decorated for at least a decade, and the room was ripe for a total and radical overhaul. The discerning owners wanted a look that was exciting and modern, as well as being elegantly chic enough for entertaining. The French doors help to give the room a continental flavor, suggesting warm sun and the use of punchy colors. However, a recently acquired slim sofa, in its basic upholsterer's muslin, also needs to be brought into this equation. Mediterranean fabrics provide a good starting point for vivid, passionate shades. Beginning with a good selection of fabric swatches all with a Spanish theme, the sofa is reupholstered in a lavishly embroidered cotton. The bold, regular motif is in keeping with the sofa's formal shape and the warm tones of the stylized flowers can be exploited throughout the room.

Above Contrast the formality of a graphic pattern with fluid detailing, like the gentle gathers on a pillow or a soft ruffle around a chair seat.

Left and Opposite The French doors, allowing in maximum light, set the tone for a light and airy scheme. Floral, check, and plain fabrics are chosen in equal measures to achieve a harmonious balance, without any one of the designs stealing a march on the others. Likewise, the strong, clear turquoise is balanced with similar expanses of cream.

Above Draperies with contrasting borders look slick and polished and brighten up plain cotton, linen, or wool. Deep shades can be contrast-lined, too.

Right Create a colorboard from a single motif by painting a square of poster board in each of the shades in the design. Then lay a sample swatch of fabric on each square; this will make it easier to determine which color feels right for the walls.

The right mix

Choosing a color scheme from a fabric can be difficult. Here the embroidered flower is made up of a number of colors, from scarlet, plaster pink, and turquoise, to cream, forest green, and gold. For impact, the living-room walls need something bold. Forest green and gold seem too traditional for a fresh, contemporary ambience while, in large quantities, red is too deep and pink too cloying. Turquoise, however, is satisfyingly serene, yet at the same time vibrant and a touch Mediterranean. The floorboards are painted vanilla to disguise the wear and tear, and to hint at a cool surface normally associated with hotter climes.

Unadorned cotton fabrics are the focus for the soft furnishings, as they are understated, crisp, and in line with the plain cotton background on the sofa. In fact, the sofa's creamy background inspired the purchase of an entire bolt of muslin from which emerged flowing full-length draperies and a reupholstered formal French antique armchair. Use plain fabrics with care in a formal setting, so that draperies do not end up resembling dust sheets, and newly minted upholstery does not look as if it is still waiting for a revamp. These drapes have been cleverly customized with ties and edging in a contrasting red cotton. A fringe of contemporary burlap enlivens the brushed-cotton stool.

Although plain fabrics and a single pattern look good, a splash of traditional check in a modern turquoise gives the entire room a razor-sharp finish. It reiterates the contemporary angles of the sofa and echoes the weave of the coir mat. It also transforms an ordinary armchair into a covetable piece of furniture with its crisp, box-pleated cover.

Opposite Less is always more: relaxed, minimal accessories give the right contemporary look. A spindly gilded lamp with a tall coolie shade, wobbly ceramics in palest cream, and unframed oils casually propped against the mantelpiece allow the colorful walls to sing out without distracting the eye. Vivid greenery or massed flowerheads all of a kind look stylish in a modern interior. Lime and red provide this room's principal accent shades.

FURNITURE

Grand or simple, each piece of furniture tells its own story. It is a composite of a designer's inspiration, cultural influences, its material make-up, and function. The older it is, the more messages and memories it carries. As its physical components become uniquely mellowed by wear and tear, it takes on more of a character of its own.

Color and light are responsible for the natural ambience of a room, but the furniture placed within it stamps a personality. A piece may be chosen for its shape, materials, or historical resonance, or to reflect a trend. Equally, a piece may choose us by being handed down through generations, or by fulfilling a practical need. However you acquire it, exploit its potential. If it has none, have no qualms about starting afresh. Beautiful furniture is often the key to a beautiful room.

SOURCES OF INSPIRATION

It is rare to start a decorating scheme without a single stick of furniture. A room filled with brand-new pieces lacks the emotional attachment most of us have for furniture that we have lived with in other settings. Weaving a scheme around constants should not be a chore but seen as a helpful structure for developing ideas. The more you consider what you have in a positive light, the more likely it is that a piece will suggest an entire decorating scheme. And if a multiplicity of paint colors and furnishing fabrics makes it hard to choose, turn to furniture as a starting point.

Suddenly, instead of colors and patterns, you are thinking in terms of hard surfaces—wood, metals, plastics—and shapes, so there is less worry about what matches what. The principles remain the same, but the focus is different. A set of 1950s kitchen chairs in sweet candy colors might set you off in a kitsch direction, or provoke a color scheme. Style and historical influences become more significant and can be interpreted more literally. A curvaceous French country armoire may set you on the road to a combination of rustic furniture and Provençal cottons. Or the elongated, strict lines of a Regency sofa may become part of an historical transformation. If they are there, exploit more subtle connections. A swirly pattern on an etched glass cabinet front might set off a motif-led scheme. If the single most stunning feature of a piece is its gigantic size, go with that, too.

Antique shops, flea markets, garage sales, salvage yards, and auctions are brilliant hunting grounds for every type and style of furniture. Start to define and refine your taste if you do not already have a specific style. This is not about getting good value or making an investment, although they are relevant, but about finding things that please and inspire you. Consider the clear, graphic lines of modern furniture, in shops and magazines. You might not want to live with such trendy pieces but their new mood might cause a subtle change of direction.

CONSIDERING FORM

Shape and size determine the way furniture works in a room; they are constants that cannot be changed. Start by considering the positive aspects of the shapes; which pieces work in harmony; and whether one of them, perhaps a wing chair, has such a strong outline that it deserves to be made a focal point. Think about how you might emphasize it. Perhaps place it centrally, where it can be admired from different angles, or range it against a wall painted in a defining color. You might even highlight the lines of a tightly upholstered piece with plain fabric and decorative studding. Do not restrict your

Opposite Look beyond the received function of a piece of furniture. Its form and spirit may suggest an alternative use. Far from looking drab, school chairs have a strong, simple outline that sits well in a fresh, minimalist scheme with pale wood flooring and white walls.

Right The more individual a piece of furniture, the more it has to contribute to a scheme that combines styles. The freehand outline of this painted headboard has rustic overtones and looks good with the casual colorwashed walls, simple bed linen, and stone floor. Yet, the combination of its random curves and an eclectic collection of bedside treasures gives the room a quirky look that transcends traditional country style.

thoughts to one room. Think about your furniture throughout the house and do not hesitate to swap pieces around to get a good balance. If all the shapes seem disparate and fail to make a great statement, seek to unify the furniture in some way. Slipcovers on a diverse selection of armchairs and sofas in a single fabric and style work wonders. Likewise, use a paintbrush on junk-shop finds and less valuable pieces.

Size should be worked with and played up, rather than despaired over. It will always be an issue if you live in a small space and have too much to cram in. Keep only furniture you really love or that is indispensably useful. If any piece is too big for its designated space, abandon any preconceptions you may have that a room needs a certain amount of equally spaced furniture in it. A tiny room with a wonderful, large bed and clothes hanging decoratively from pegs will be more stimulating than the same space stuffed with a smaller, nondescript bed and a chest of drawers. If you have a large room with little furniture, think about arranging it in groups in order to fill the space, paying attention to scale so that varying heights distract attention from small proportions. Or, perhaps you might invest in one huge piece that will dominate the space.

Look afresh at the textures, colors, and properties of each piece of furniture. If a table is grand and made from a beautiful wood, it should become a focal point. But a crumbling and faded paint surface or scratched gilding can be appealing, too. You might want to highlight an old chair by collecting around it several similarly "distressed" pieces—a mirror, a side table, a lampstand. If none of your pieces has a special texture, consider faking it. Add contemporary laminate to an old table, or gently distress a new pine hutch with a paint effect. Your choice of fabric pattern may change the character of upholstered furniture. Modern fabrics give an unusual twist to more traditional shapes, and a classic chintz on a space-age shape will look innovative.

Above Cracked and peeling paint, with its glimpses of partly exposed color, can itself be the inspiration for a decorating scheme. A simply furnished bedroom becomes a restful retreat with only a rustic armoire and iron bedstead.

Opposite Look for elements that will soften the hard edges of a modern interior. Chairs of shiny white plastic with tubular-steel legs might have had an overly cool influence in this contemporary kitchen, but the matte gray linoleum floor, filmy curtain, and wooden table all help to diffuse any hint of clinical modernism.

CONSIDERING FUNCTION

Furniture is essentially functional, however gorgeous. Think how a room will be used and what wear and tear individual pieces might receive. The function of a room may demand practical features from its furniture, such as storage space, or a large workstation in a home office. Consider alternative uses for your existing furniture. Would the dining table be better used as a desk, or the bulky wardrobe in the spare room be more useful, and look more spectacular, as a food cupboard in the kitchen? Add various inventive detailing so that it is beautiful to look at, too. Think laterally about the received use of each item. A large mirror makes a stunningly original headboard, or a one-off antique dining chair can become a pretty and serviceable nightstand. But if the shape of a piece of furniture overshadows its function, locate it where it can be seen to the best advantage.

USING FURNITURE: THE CHOICES

Furniture is a powerful decorating tool and very different effects can be achieved simply by unifying or juxtaposing the various

pieces. Linking factors are easiest to work with. You may already have started the process unconsciously by combining furniture of a certain historical period simply because you like the way it looks together. A collection of modern pieces, each by a different designer, might share translucent plastics in indulgent colors as their common denominator, and other shades and textiles could provide more links.

The visual tension arising from unusual juxtapositions of elements that create surprise and stimulation is easily engineered by mixing disparate styles of furniture. But do not make odd combinations just for the sake of it.

Mixing grand and simple furniture also offers potential for altering mood. Introduce a weathered garden chair into a living room to challenge too formal a look. Connecting it visually to something else in the room, perhaps an equally battered metal chandelier, will help to anchor it in the scheme. Experiment with a contrast of fabric styles on upholstered furniture. You could use a cheap lilac cotton duck on real Louis XV dining chairs, thus introducing a lighthearted element into a formal setting. Create a more casual feel by the way furniture is placed. Prop rather than hang large mirrors; push a lovely sleigh bed into the middle of a bedroom. Always try to mix furniture to look as if a room has evolved naturally.

ACCENTING WITH FURNITURE

Unless a very modern or rustic style has stripped a piece of furniture to bare essentials, most pieces have elements that can be teased out and highlighted. Discreet little legs on upholstered furniture can be painted a brilliant color for extra zip, or the back of a glass-fronted display cabinet might be wallpapered in an extravagantly patterned design. Such accent details can send subtle shock waves through an otherwise unified scheme. Accenting can be kept as simple as a contrasting texture or shape, such as using a square brushed-steel mirror to break up the soft curvy lines of a room dominated by upholstery.

Above Traditional furniture revitalized with creative upholstery can radically alter the look of a room. Classic Louis XV chairs, painted mint green and covered in a saffron- and cranberry-colored floral print, look quite at home in a period interior, while bringing to it a light touch of humor. Consider which pieces of your furniture could be transformed, and take risks.

Opposite A piece of furniture can be customized to disguise its shortcomings, or to give it an individual, quirky new look. This bleached wooden hutch has been revamped with the addition of rope handles and studded metal panels. Save customizing for the final stages of redecorating a room, so that your detailing can tie the piece into your scheme.

MAKING IT HAPPEN

Unless you have been blessed with an extraordinarily vivid imagination, you will have to shift your furniture around to discover what works best. Redecorating a room is a marvelous opportunity to consider the space afresh because the existing order will already be disturbed. It could also be the time to jettison any piece that does not work. If possible, take everything out of the room, and reintroduce it piece by piece. You might realize that the two sofas you had facing each other give more scope for separate task areas placed back to back. If furniture is your decorative starting point, decide what colors and textiles work with it. When you are putting together your colorboard, include photographs of the key pieces of furniture, with measurements, so that you can see how the various elements will work in unison.

Inevitably, you will want to search for at least one new piece of furniture to build on a theme or to replace an abandoned article. Knowing your sources is essential. Visit and revisit shops and auctions, and eventually something will catch your eye. If you are looking for a specific period piece, find out who in your area specializes in that type of furniture. Consider reproduction items and mix them judiciously with authentic pieces. The classified ads in interior design magazines are a good source of unusual or specialist furniture. Most furniture stores that make to order can adjust a sofa design to the size you require, elongate a table to your dimensions, or make whatever you want in a different combination of woods. Working with a furniture designer on a unique piece is not necessarily ruinously expensive. If you see a one-off antique piece that is just right except for its color, size, or price, photograph it, and then find a craftsman to make it. Consider buying furniture from secondhand shops and repainting, re-covering, or adding unusual details, such as wheels on a coffee table, or sanding a cheap piece of pine furniture and painting it a cool, matte color.

Opposite The furniture in a room will affect its look far more than the color of the walls. Always consider scale and proportion as well as style. A formal arrangement is saved from stuffiness by the inclusion of both fitted upholstery and relaxed, contemporary slipcovers.

Above A gloriously proportioned wardrobe from a more opulent age need not look out of place in a small house. Keep other elements to a minimum, colors pale, textiles plain, and let the ornate piece become the center of attention.

A Flea-Market Find

An antique chair, carved and painted, exudes a feeling of frivolity.

The curvy legs and nipped-in waist are suggestive of feminine charm,

while the faded gilding hints at the decadence of a lost age. Placed

in a high-ceilinged bathroom next to the sweeping curves of a roll-topped

bath, it signals the starting point of a glamorous transformation,

where the richness of gilding and the promise of luxury collide.

Above The appeal of an antique piece of furniture is multi-stranded. Explore its shape, makeup, style, and period for the chance to develop a decorative lead.

Right Equipped with the beautiful basics of a generous roll-topped bath and pedestal sink, combined with lofty proportions, a bathroom can reinvent itself time and time again.

Opposite Understated peach walls and a gleaming wooden floor give way to a wash of lilac and touches of gilding for a glamorous, feminine revamp.

Tiled and modern for a short, sharp sluice, or a temple of indulgence for hours of pampering—a bathroom can be many things. With its double-hung window, gilded armchair, and screen, this bathroom was perfect for a romantic transformation, but its parchment walls and dark floorboards gave it a gloomy air. The Parisian chic of the gilded chair conjures up visions of a vast apartment with French doors, marble floors, lace curtains, and a hint of perfume. But to avoid a clumsy pastiche, this look should be adapted, rather than copied. Rich, dark shades are far too theatrical; instead combine gilt with serene, pretty tones—eau-de-Nil, melon, and palest lilac—for something that is refreshing yet decadent. The lilac on the walls means that

the chestnut floorboards do not fit in with the scheme. The radical decision to lay faux black-and-white marble tiles clearly sets the scene for a Parisian-style bathroom, but with thoroughly modern plumbing.

Left Precious details count. Here, a slim lavender grosgrain ribbon finishes off an upholstered chair seat, echoing the ribbed cotton upholstery used on the armchair and screen.

Above A self-indulgent bathroom calls for heady perfumes, luxurious lotions, and dreamy, scented candles. Remove favorite products from more urbane packaging. Decant brilliantly coloured oils and bubble baths into antique glass bottles, pour bath salts into crystal bowls, and keep less beautiful essentials firmly behind the medicine cabinet door. A gilded soap dish and an etched glass toothbrush holder will transform everyday ablutions into something special.

Opposite For the ultimate, tactile bathroom, start by assembling fabrics in place of tiles, trimmings instead of faucets. Abandon preconceptions about what can and cannot be used. Sheeny textures, airy voile, smooth, pure cotton, and a dash of bobbly braid lie at the heart of a decadent, comfortable bathroom retreat.

Salon style

The secret of an indulgent bathroom is to sort out the behind-the-scenes practicalities first. There is nothing romantic about water-marked satin or damask wallpaper lifting from the wall. Think about surfaces. Floors need to be water-repellent and fabrics splash-resistant; you do not need to have tiles, but marble backsplashes and painted walls are better than wallpaper, which has a tendency to peel. Good heating and ventilation are also essential.

Choosing the perfect shade of lilac paint sets the tone. Classically pretty shades, spreading through the spectrum from lavender to rose, have a surprising variance. There is no such

Right Use soaps for dashes of dense, brilliant color. Gather them in a glass bowl and use them as ever-changing accent shades.

Below A chair and plump pillows to relax against take the bathroom to new, indulgent heights. Fluffy big towels, towel warmer and a luxurious velvet dressing gown are the essential ingredients of the perfect bathtime treat.

color as pure lilac; instead versions range from blue and pink to gray. What may seem like a true lilac on a paint swatch can look overpowering as a test patch on a wall. You will find a pearly gray lilac has a fresh, light feel to it. White woodwork would look too bright with all the gilded and marbled surfaces. So experiment with alternatives, looking through the palest pastel shades. Here, an unlikely but beautiful whisper of plaster pink eggshell enhances the moldings and the bath. For a grandiose flourish, the sides of the bath can also be painted in gold.

Luscious textiles are at the heart of a sensual bathroom, though sheeny cottons are preferable to real silk, which can be marked and spoiled by water. The armchair and screen are lifted from shabby chic to contemporary baroque with a fine rib-cotton upholstery in vibrant lime and amethyst. Provided there is an efficient screen at the window, such as a blind or opaque glass, curtains can be used to maximum effect. To achieve a sophisticated salon style, this Roman shade has been made from an embroidered antique linen sheet, and a filmy voile curtain is draped elegantly over a holdback. Lace panels or printed voile are also excellent bathroom fabrics, and a skilled window-shade maker will be able to stiffen them gently while retaining their translucent quality.

If there is plenty of room, a bathroom can also accommodate comfortable furniture that will allow you to relax. An armchair, a side table to hold a drink, and an armoire crammed with towels and scented linens all turn a practical room into a glorious retreat; you could even create a dressing room if you have the space. But pay attention to style. The select cluster of gilded furniture in this room is enough; adding more pieces would destroy the equilibrium of the look. Instead, a marble-topped side table, a curly

Left A simple length of voile, trimmed with pompom fringe and artfully draped, creates a luxurious new look. Experiment with other textiles in the bathroom. An antique linen sheet, clipped in front of a practical, clear shower curtain, looks infinitely more inviting than the squeaky plastic alternative.

iron towel holder, a metal wall sconce, and a rose-carved painted mirror continue the mood of decorative, indulgent treasures, gathered together for their antique appeal.

A modern twist

A period look, however lightly reinterpreted, needs a contemporary edge. Some rooms glory in the mix of antique and modern furniture, but the contrast is much more subtle here. Slick cosmetic packaging—silvery canisters and cool, conical-shaped bottles—look stylish, as do fresh white towels trimmed with zingy lime. Pretty colors like lilac need acid overtones to define them as fashionable

rather than prissy. The lime pompom fringe on the curtain and the startlingly bright lime lozenge soaps, mixed with brilliant turquoise and amethyst, all stop the bathroom from looking too pretty.

A decadent, decorated room benefits from plain and simple undercurrents. The smart black-and-white checkerboard flooring balances the gilded splendor. But so, too, does the crisp monochrome cotton found in a Swedish floral print, which has been used to upholster the little gilt chair, and as a scatter pillow on the giant Baroque armchair. Used judiciously, black and white are excellent equalizers, toning down color and injecting a little restraint.

POSSESSIONS

Favorite things, possessions, keepsakes, and treasures frequently have no other purpose except to impart immense pleasure. These are the objects we might momentarily hold or glance at to recharge a memory or appreciate an aesthetic quality. It is human nature to surround ourselves with things we love. And precious need not mean expensive. Too often, such treasures only come out of their boxes at the end of the decorating process to be fitted into the scheme instead of being part of the whole. They are often muddled up with out-of-date accessories, disliked presents, and mistaken buys. So, be clear about what you do love. Does it tell a story, or does it inspire you? Does it impart color, or is it quirky or pretty enough to become a central focus in a room?

SOURCES OF INSPIRATION

Do not assume that as soon as you start looking, objects you have had around for years will mysteriously reveal a secret side bursting to be exploited. It is not that simple. Exploring favorite things for a decorative starting point is more a lateral way of thinking; it should be fun and slightly frivolous. Search through cupboards, look afresh at ornaments and pictures, reconsider pictures you have not had framed, cracked china, and family heirlooms. A pattern with inspiring colors on a faded quilt may cry out to be part of a shabby chic style. This is more a process of looking at what is around you over time, whether at home, in a store, or at an antiques fair, and learning to see hidden facets that can be drawn out and developed. Hone your taste so you are able to analyze and react instinctively, having the confidence to buy that chance find.

Think, too, about the concept of a possession. It is not necessarily a decorative object or an artifact. A square of translucent blue soap, clear and perfect, sitting on a chrome

Above Left A favorite set of prints can set the style of a room. A group of images in identical frames and hung in a tight block looks impressive as it creates the illusion of being one big picture.

Above Ideas for customizing a display cabinet arise from the nature of a collection. Here, porcelain has suggested an outsize scallop on open shelving. Chinoiserie vases prompted chair slipcovers in green-and-white toile; and the abstract motif of rosy sprigs on the plates is reflected in a cotton lawn cloth.

USING POSSESSIONS : THE CHOICES

The nature of precious things is as diverse as their owners, but as a general principle, consider your treasure in terms of color, texture, shape, and pattern. To see familiar items afresh, take them out of context, away from where you are used to seeing them, and mix them up on a table. If a picture appeals and the frame does not, discard the frame and let the image stand alone. Regard everything with a gimlet eye, and put aside anything you do not love.

Items that are intended to please visually–paintings, decorative china, a needlepoint pillow–can be interpreted in much the same way as, say, the designs within a fabric. Consider the myriad strands of pattern, theme, and color. It will be your own private joke to include the original item in the finished room. Few will guess its importance as an inspirational starting point, but you can still enjoy the connection, and the object.

The process will be utterly different if your inspiration is more abstract, items culled from nature or an autumn walk, such as a collection of pearly shells. You might interpret these things literally by devising a color scheme that reminds you of the beach, the changing light, the sandy textures. Or you might concentrate in a more abstract manner on the texture of rough seed pods and twisted branches picked up in a forest. The resulting decorative scheme may only be subtly linked, revealing itself in a penchant for dark woods, nubby textures, and a more casual placing of furniture. The mood you remember from that autumn walk will always be at the forefront of your mind when you sit in the room, and that is what counts most.

So possessions can hold the key to a direct color scheme; or they may influence the look of the room subtly. They can take center stage as a stunning focal point. Perhaps you have a richly framed portrait, your favorite possession both emotionally and visually. Of course, you may take its colors and weave a scheme around them, perhaps using contrast

dish, holds a glimmer of inspiration for decorating a bathroom using cubist shapes, transparent surfaces, and cooling aqua colors. A bowl on a kitchen shelf, crammed with rough string, manila envelopes, and household candles may hold the essence of your next kitchen scheme. Try putting together a collection of colors and textures that please and stir you.

Inspiration for displaying possessions may arise from something as obvious as visiting museums and art galleries, where the sole purpose is to show an artifact to its best advantage. Look at the space around a picture, the way it is hung, the grouping of objects. Can this be reinterpreted at home?

as a means of highlighting it. Somewhere in the picture there may be a flash of unexpected color that could be used on the wall where it will hang. Or you may choose barely-there shades and matte textures, so that the room effectively becomes a blank canvas for one, or several, pictures. Equally, consider ways of displaying the portrait to direct attention to it. Hang it center stage, alone over a bare mantelpiece. Or work out where a significant shaft of sunshine falls and hang your picture in its own natural spotlight.

Collections with a common theme, or linked visual appeal, can also spark off a room scheme. They might be faded, antique finds lovingly collected over time—handpainted plates,

wooden shoe lasts, or antique maps. Or your tastes could be more contemporary and transitory, changing from one month to the next, from a set of a particular artist's black-and-white postcards to a huge glass bowl filled to the brim with autumn leaves as the season turns. Think how best to use and highlight your collection. You could develop a theme by searching out a map motif fabric, painting the walls in parchment shades, and hanging maps for maximum effect. More subtly, a single handpainted rose on one of your plates might loosely connect with a pretty chintz for a sofa, or a dusky pink for the walls. Or if your collections are likely to change often, then deliberately opt for neutrals

Opposite A favorite possession may have only a subtle and almost indiscernible link to the finished scheme. Minimalist cylindrical glass vases inspired this worldly scheme, with its strong interplay of parallel lines and neutral colors.

Right A painting can inspire a fresh new scheme. Analyze the colors used to see why they work together. The tonal variations, texture of brush-strokes on canvas, and lavender blues in this painting have all been alluded to in the handpainted canvas chair covers. The yellow greens are picked up in a bowl of fresh pears, and the neutral tones repeated in the bleached wood of a contemporary table and the sisal floor matting.

or monochrome shades with few distracting patterns, which will allow for that transitoriness. Deep, pale-wood picture frames can hold shells one week and sheets of old music the next; tall glass vases can show off textured collections of ribbon or string; a low, simple shelf running right around the room is ideal for displaying anything from new snapshots to treasures from a trip abroad.

The final style of a room is inextricably linked with the grouping of favorite objects, whether you have decided to take your decorative inspiration directly from those same objects, or whether you are putting them together right at the end. Tap into the current vogue for simplicity.

If you cannot decide whether to set out an entire collection of creamware pitchers or just the most beautiful one, restrict yourself to the latter. The calmness of one may set you thinking about trying out a clutter-free environment, with barely-there colors and minimal furniture. The way you display things will also dictate the ambience and finished look of a room, be it casual or chic. Think about your natural style. Do you prefer a just-put-down cluster of precious objects, or is symmetry important to you? The latter will be more in keeping with a designed, ordered environment and decorative style. Cross barriers and try out each look to see which feels right.

THE PRACTICALITIES

Favorite possessions deserve to be admired, not just by you but by friends, visitors, and family. So, do not distance your favorite things by hiding them in glass cabinets or high up on shelves. Most rooms have architectural features that should be considered first, from a deep windowsill to a mantelpiece, an alcove to a picture rail. Display things where they can be seen at close range or where they can be picked up and admired. If you do need to devote furniture to display, keep it simple. A low tabletop, an open-shelved cabinet, or a sturdy wooden chair frequently looks more casual as a vehicle for display than do purpose-built display cabinets or shelves. But, think practically, too. Are children going to knock things off. Does that same low tabletop also need to hold newspapers, or drinks?

An important possession may have dictated the entire layout and scheme of your room, but think also about ways to enhance all the smaller objects. Tricks include gathering colored glass in front of a window to glow in the sunlight; or giving significance to family snapshots by framing them identically and grouping them together on one wall. Instead of hanging pictures from hooks, trail them from long velvet ribbons, or industrial chains. Cram pebbles from the beach into a shallow glass bowl filled with water to highlight their natural hues.

We can deliberately style special things in a room to get the look we want. Once the decoration is complete and furniture is in place, gather together all your accessories and experiment with them. Live with your new arrangements for a while. Tinker with them until they look right. Displays will be seen afresh if altered from time to time. Prop up pictures on a mantelpiece; arrange unexpected combinations of old and new. Clutter a surface, then take everything away except a vase of flowers. Does a lack of things seem clinical or is it a pleasant relief? Remember that less is often more. Too much clutter can kill a carefully thought-out scheme. And the more space left around one special object, the more dramatic its impact will be.

Opposite Focus attention on a large or conspicuous item by giving it lots of space, as if it were on display in a gallery. This whimsical birdcage has a wall to itself, with furniture and styling around it kept to an absolute minimum.

Above A glass-fronted cabinet, filled with favorite things, needs to be accessible, so that everyone can enjoy the items within. Leave one of the doors enticingly open, as if inviting closer inspection. Keep the display relaxed and random, changing the objects from time to time. Think about focusing attention on the cabinet. The contrast of a white-painted frame set against a midnight blue wall makes this one instantly attractive.

A Chic Fashion Accessory

A decorative fashion accessory—whether an impulse luxury buy or rediscovered in a closet—can inspire in unique and surprising ways, not least because it is so often rich in glamour and detail. Subtly shaded and finely stitched, this pair of soft kid gloves from a Paris flea market suggests simple elegance, smooth textures, and a lavender-gray color palette—just right for a city living room in need of a decorative fillip.

These beautiful gloves offer inspiration in three directions. Their sophisticated color can be the starting point for a palette of grays of varying hues—colors strong enough to make a statement, but not so dark as to be austere. Their elegance and antiquity can be matched with sympathetic furniture styles and ornate accessories. And finally, the soft sheen of the leather, combined with its top-stitching, highlights a need for sensuous, indulgent fabrics. These are the beginnings, but it is necessary to take into account the room itself—in particular its day-long brightness and the beauty of the original window shutters. It is important, too, not to ignore the potential challenge of changing existing features—how to deal, for example, with the honey-colored floorboards which are at odds with a silver-toned palette. Finally, consider any large elements that you choose to retain. Here a striking Biedermeier sofa is intended as a focal point in the room.

Above The gray of a pair of gloves is reinterpreted for a room scheme in tones of dove, pearl, and lavender.

Opposite A barely-there, neutral shade—like gray—is as valid a starting point as splashier colors.
For more depth, explore neutrals in terms of light and dark tones.

Left Tall ceilings, original window paneling, and good natural light give this room a head start, as there are no obvious flaws that need to be disguised.

A tone on tone palette

To use the gray of the gloves as an exact color reference would almost certainly have resulted in too shadowy a color. Instead, pale gray paint for walls and woodwork sets the scene, selected from shades of antiqued white rather than proper grays. Now the palette needs fleshing out with fabrics: some luxuriously silky in order to add sophistication, and others with a textural twist to add bite to the one-color scheme.

A chic, silvery crepe satin is ideal for draped window swags, and two paler silky stripes sit well as pillow covers and upholstery. Alongside the crepe satin, two textural crunchy matte cottons act as a foil: one to line a tailored throw, the other to make into a second set of pillows. Although this completes the interplay of gray tones, some gentle spicing up is needed. This is achieved through a splash of pattern and a hint of extra color. Here, the answer is a sumptuous embroidered brocade which elevates the Biedermeier sofa to glamorous new heights; while, for the stool, a tiny gingham in fresh lavender adds "zip."

Above Slinky satins, crisp cottons, and lavish embroidery, all in understated shades of palest gray, lavender, and ecru, create the basis for a sophisticated, salon style.

Right Extend a textural story through to the accessories. Where there is sheen on fabrics, look for equivalents in hard surfaces. Translucent glass and shimmering silvery finishes are all complementary.

Opposite Formal rooms call for serious, elegant pieces of furniture. It is possible to draw together different styles by searching for thematic links. The boxy armchair and Gustavian console work in tandem, for example, because of their narrow, elegant legs; and even the paneled detail on the table is echoed in the silky stripe of the upholstery.

Glamorous highlights

In a room planned as a grown-up retreat, mood is everything. A few well-chosen pieces of dark wood furniture will introduce grandeur, as will tailored upholstery, highlighted minimally with studding and self-welting. In general, sophistication is best maintained by an absence of frills, so the draped swags are kept crisp, and the slippery throw unadorned.

A chic, salon style like this also requires discipline when considering what is out on show. Piles of magazines and overstuffed bookshelves are anathema and should either be banished to another room or concealed behind storage that blends elegantly with the other furniture. Only then can decorative items be properly planned for display. Silver candlesticks and pewter echo the silvery gray palette; instead of pictures, etched wine glasses and mirrors play up the abundance of sunlight; and the vibrant fuchsia pink trace in the embroidered brocade is picked out in a vase full of hyacinths. Their heady perfume, combined with scented candles, provides an indulgent ambience just right for, say, an evening's entertaining.

Opposite In a dining room setting, look to china and table linen to echo decorative accenting that has already been established. Pearly bone handles, ornate silver detailing, crunchy quilted cloths, and fine linen build on the translucence, sparkle, and silvery colors already in place.

Left Fabric design can heavily influence the look of an upholstered piece. A stylized floral motif accentuates the curved, formal lines of the Biedermeier sofa.

Above A flawless and tailored room should have crisp window treatments. The sinuous drapes of swags are not only perfectly in keeping with the mood, but also show off the original window paneling. In a more relaxed room, a plain recessed shade or a contrasting color on the paneling will suffice to dress the window while capitalizing on its glorious proportions.

Colorful Collection

A collection of beautiful objects, lovingly amassed over the years, can generate ideas that might define and direct the look of an entire room. This glorious collection of glass provides a wealth of inspiration for a room scheme. The exhilarating extremes of color, the eccentric shapes, and the mix of clear and opaque glass encourage an experimental, artistic treatment for what was previously a plain country living room.

Above A collection of glass vases is unified by a common theme, but it is often the idiosyncrasies, the clashes of texture and form, that provoke a more thoughtful interpretation.

Right Take an open-minded approach to architectural features, and do not let them dominate a design decision.

Opposite The plain fireplace in this rustic location did not have to mean a country cottage look. Rather its simplicity inspires a contemporary scheme in bold colors, and a confident mixture of classic and modern furniture styles.

The vivid shades of this glassware collection do not provide the basis for a color scheme in the conventional sense. A combination of tangerine, jade, deep purple, and turquoise, transposed literally onto walls and furniture, would be eccentric in the extreme. But this collection does provide the inspiration for using strong colors together, for playing with chance contrasts, just as they occur naturally within the collection. The impact of multicolored glass vases ranged against an off-white wall can be re-created in a room using bold blocks of color combined with more stable neutrals. Considered in this more abstract vein, color can be used as a tool to define space.

This living room had little to recommend it architecturally; there was a low ceiling, a concrete floor, and a very plain fireplace. The room also lacked atmosphere so color is used to give the room a more quirky spirit.

Left Create a working sample-board in the room you are decorating. Start off with a notebook and fill it with experimental sketches, exploring the room from varying angles, adding paint chips and small swatches of fabric. As you narrow down the choices, start to paint tiny sections of wall using sample pots, then pin up fabric favorites to check the effects of light on the different materials and the interplay of texture.

A balancing act

For the color scheme, four major shades are selected from the glassware: a vivid jade, a coppery blue-green, a canary yellow, and a deep purple. Before applying the color, the space is turned into what amounts to a blank canvas: the walls are painted antique white and a floor is laid with pale oak woodblock. Next, each section of wall is painted either jade, blue-green, or yellow, a treatment that both echoes the glassware and suggests a painterly environment. Each panel of color is deliberately positioned next to an unassuming feature such as the fireplace or the alcove, which instantly injects character where none existed before. Finally, for a more textured effect, the wet paint is drybrushed, creating an impression of old plaster.

The bold panels of wall color need to be balanced within the room with at least one other element in a similarly strong tone. Here, deep purple is used, which is incorporated into the scheme in the matte brushed cotton upholstery of the Art Deco furniture. The same fabric would have been too dark for the mahogany daybed, so pale green cotton with a seedling motif is used instead. This bridges the gap between bolds and neutrals seamlessly, and the pattern thematically hints at the garden just outside without detracting from the color story within.

Blocks and splashes

This scheme aims to surprise, so unusual accent colors and the way they are used are key elements. The juxtaposition of a bright turquoise glass next to an amethyst vase makes a striking contrast on the shelf; this contrast is daringly used as upholstery welting, too. The chartreuse of a handblown vase is reinterpreted as a scatter pillow, while the singing lime of another is painted as a panel on the wall. As the pinkish-mauve garden flowers in the vase look so good, scatter pillows and a bolster are made in the same color.

Below Use accessories to repeat the basic tones of a color scheme. Scatter pillows with simple styling in strong shades and neutrals echo the panels on the walls.

Left When a collection has inspired an entire room, it is much more fun if it is center stage in the finished space. Colored glass always looks spectacular on glass shelves, but if there is no suitable alcove, consider adding them to a recessed window. Taking pieces from the collection and placing them around the room makes everything much less formal. Some of the glassware in this collection is rearranged on the mantelpiece and then filled with flowers for a less gallery-like feel.

NATURAL LIGHT

Simultaneously powerful and subtle, natural light awakens us, colors our feelings, and leaves us at the end of the day. We take it for granted, yet its gradual shift in depth and quality is constantly shaping our mood and the interiors we inhabit. The play of light can make a room tranquil and welcoming, dramatic, or gloomy. Without it there would be none of the silhouettes, contrasts, or sunbeams that enhance the appeal of any interior. It affects the colors on our walls, our carefully chosen textures, and is the one natural element that must be taken into account when planning a room. Artists, photographers, interior designers, and architects all try to capture it, but for everyone observation is the key. Watch what light does throughout the day (and seasons), and then exploit it to the full.

SOURCES OF INSPIRATION

We are all aware that naturally sunny rooms uplift us and gloomy ones do not. A sudden burst of sunshine warms and animates a room, the power of its light influencing a look and creating an ambience. And the fall and patterns of natural light can be explored and tapped into as a rich source of inspiration for decorating. Cool, diffuse light may suggest chalky, pale colors. Sun on square windowpanes might spark a checkerboard theme, while shady spaces might call for heavy textiles you are not usually drawn to. Let light guide you creatively, then work with it.

Locate the light source in your room and try to gauge its quality and intensity. Observe it at lunchtime and late afternoon. Enjoy the sun setting, watch the shadows. Is it a morning or an evening room? Is the light right for its current function? Look at the way light comes through the windows. Does it create attractive shadows on a wall, are there powerful sunbeams that act as natural spotlights, or is the light always diffuse? If the room stays somber even on a sunny day, does this bother you or might you capitalize on it? Do you find very strong sunlight distracting? Any of these things could be a starting point for the way you decorate. Pin down the mood created by the light and keep it in mind.

There are numerous ways of manipulating light within the home, and the effects can be striking. Observe it on a grand scale in historic houses or public buildings. Think of light streaming through leaded-glass windows and onto the floor, the cool tranquility of a shady old church, the patterns of shadows cast from high windows in a library. Glance through art and photography books, focusing on light, shade, and silhouettes, and observe how it can heighten color to surreal depths, or knock it dead. Look at interiors in magazines. Focus on the play of light in interiors of different styles. Mediterranean houses may suggest unusual ideas for coping with strong directional light; or use colors other than neutrals.

Left The addition of a skylight or solarium-style roof is more structural, yet extremely effective in opening up a shady space. Plan your decoration to work with the direction of the light. The creamy brown walls, stone floor, and dark woods in this sunroom look intensely dramatic cut through with slivers of sunlight.

Right Pale, creamy tones and a minimal amount of furniture in an attic bedroom make the most of little sunlight, as does a translucent sheer curtain caught back from an iron rod. A small or inset window requires special attention. Think about what is most appropriate, both to maximize light and to tie it in with the intended style of the room.

USING LIGHT: BRIGHT ROOMS

Sun-filled rooms with ample windows are often the ones most used in the house. They generate a relaxed mood but encourage activity and are ideal as kitchens, playrooms, and living rooms. What does a surfeit of light suggest to you in terms of colors and textures? Do you want to exploit its sunny nature or cool things down? Do you want to introduce an element of sophistication or retain a casual feel? All light needs to be contained and directed, and your window treatments will significantly influence the style of a room.

For a sunny feel, look at colors that mimic and work with the sun's warm tones. This does not mean strong, bright colors; an excess of sunlight can fade and negate them. Think instead of the tones and shades that sunlight itself casts: soft tangerines, butter yellows, rosy pinks, and the duskiest of reds. Even on cloudy days, such shades continue to suggest sunlight, and need only a hint of the real thing to bring a room to life. Consider, too, the impact of reflection. Wood or natural-fiber floors in honey tones are more mellow than shiny

Above Even without strong sunlight, an all-white room is unfailingly bright. But such rooms need textures if they are to avoid a hint of chilliness in winter. Matte floorboards and woven cotton covers in white look and feel warm. Translucent shades offer some control of light by directing and screening the rays. The flicker of a real fire is a welcome contrast on darker days.

Opposite Rather than attempting to compensate for the lack of light in a basement, use rich, somber colors to build on its intrinsic qualities and create a cozy atmosphere. This pale charcoal, taupe, and white bedroom looks serene and inviting. Its modernist detailing draws attention away from the dearth of natural lighting. Fresh white bed linen and paintwork suggest highlights where none actually exist.

whitewashed boards. Likewise, lean toward matte, textured fabrics that will absorb the sunlight—soft cottons, linens, and loose weaves rather than sheeny material. Small patterns have to work harder if there is a lot of light bouncing around. Try a large-scale design that will not be nearly as overpowering when light and shade are playing over walls or curtains.

The need to cool down a bright room calls not for deep, somber shades, which might look dirty in the full glare of the sun, but for calming colors. Take a tip from hot countries where shady interiors are painted in tones of blue and green, from azure to midnight, seafoam to aqua. Stripes, whether on walls or upholstery, give an illusion of light and shade, and can cool things down visually. A dappled or distressed paint finish on the walls would suggest a play of shadows where they do not fall naturally.

Use light to influence mood and style naturally. To play up a sunny feel, choose curtain treatments that will diffuse the light. The most obvious, but classically simple, solution is to mix conventional lined draperies with roll-up shades in the sheerest voile. You can take down the draperies in the height of summer and leave the shades in place, or hang temporary summer "curtains." There are numerous floaty textiles available that can be simply sewn into hemmed rectangles and attached to an existing pole using café clips. Unlined Indian cottons in hot colored stripes, simple florals, loose-weave linens, and rough burlap in neutral or deeper shades all look wonderful. Sheers have traditionally been available in white and neutrals, but now come in patterned designs, from floral to colored checks, and look very pretty billowing in a gentle breeze. If you have deep-colored walls, experiment with shades made from sheer cotton in a color to match the walls. Pulled down during the day, they will positively glow with color.

The play of dark and light, slanting shadows, and dramatic contrasts may have inspired your desire to cool down a room. Think about using roll-up shades with blackout lining; classic, neutral shades made from unbleached linen; or wooden Venetian blinds. Pull them halfway down to create dramatic slants of light or blocks of dark and shade across walls and floor. In eighteenth- or nineteenth-century houses with double-hung windows, consider reinstating authentic internal, wooden shutters that fold across the panes. Shutters are brilliant for engineering pools of light and shade, and often look best without draperies. For more organic light patterns, consider growing a creeper around a window so that it throws pretty shadows on the wall as the sun swings around. You could allow it to cover a large part of a bathroom window as a natural screen, and an odd tendril escaping inside will look charming.

Not all bright rooms will benefit from direct sunlight. Some have a colder, more diffuse northern light; or light may filter through frosted glass panes installed to provide privacy or conceal an unpleasant view. This bright but restrained light brings opportunities for playing with softer, more subtle shades. Where harsh yellow sunshine might have bleached them to obscurity, ice blues, grays, and lichen green can take on a restful tranquility when used in bright cool light. Use them in layers of differing tones, for walls, floors, and upholstery; the all-over wash of color will give an illusion of soft, constant light. Add touches of off-white to suggest gentle highlights if they are naturally lacking. An all-white room could look spectacular, but keep shapes and textures soft and welcoming to avoid any hint of clinical unfriendliness. Shadow play in a neutral room can be particularly fascinating; think of the varying tones of a sepia photo as you experiment.

USING LIGHT : DARKER ROOMS

Suggest painting a dark room in inky blue or mushroom, and most people think you are crazy. But if you are faced with one or a series of gloomy spaces, perhaps a narrow hallway and staircase, a back bedroom, or a basement, it can make sense to accept and work with the somber tones. Look at a seventeenth-century Dutch interior painting with its pools of light, deep colors and contrasting checkerboard floors, and you will see there is grandeur in dark rooms.

If you accept that your space does not have a sunny ambience, you can enjoy choosing colors to promote serenity or create a cozy element of retreat: earthy neutrals, sand, stone, dappled shades of forest green; or deep sea turquoise and aqua for an underwatery feel. Flat, matte walls will probably work better than busy wallpaper, and look good with a textured and patterned rug. For contrast and highlights, choose a creamy neutral rather than stark white. Use blocks around the room—in picture frames, scatter pillows, an armchair, or a lavish throw. To take things darker, introduce heavy wood furniture; or steer a middle course using blond wood or colorwashed pieces. In such a scheme, windows and the

amount of light they allow through become less important. Add to the rich ambience by hanging simple but heavily textured draperies in a tone to match the walls.

On balance, you may want to make your room as light as possible and this could lead you back to softer, paler shades. Surfaces that impart a subtle sheen, reflect or bounce light, or let it stream through, will all help to create a more vibrant environment. Glass-topped and plastic furniture, gloss paint, large mirrors, rakish chandeliers, or even mirror balls for the trendy, will all capture rays of light.

Go for pale-colored shades that still provide an effective screen at night, or those with punched holes that allow sunshine through. Use flat voile screens to filter light yet provide privacy from the street. Keep essential curtains pale and unlined. Cream and off-white linen or canvas can suggest sun where there is none. Similarly, keep flooring as light as possible. Consider bleached, pickled, or whitewashed floorboards; pale, gray-toned linoleum; or pastel checkerboards.

However you choose to use natural light, make major changes before you decorate. What about a wall of glass bricks; stainless steel in a kitchen or a modern interior, or fewer internal doors? Sandblasted or etched glass obviates the need for light-restricting curtains.

MAKING IT HAPPEN

If quality of light is your starting point, it will lead logically to color and fabric. Consider the physical effects of colors and patterns and observe them at varying times, imagining how light may alter them through the seasons.

The position of furniture also affects the play of light. A sparsely furnished room, with plenty of space around pieces, gives a fresh feel. Think about materials, not only light-refracting ones like plastic and glass, but also

slim-legged cane furniture, wrought-iron garden chairs, or glistening chrome and aluminum. Look at translucent materials, from blow-up plastic armchairs to the colorful polypropylene favored by modern designers. Heavy, dense, but comfortable furniture helps to create a richly warm and intimate interior, and can be placed so as to produce deep shadows or strong silhouettes.

Whatever window treatment you settle on, you will need to hang voiles, unlined fabrics, and shade textiles up at the light source, watching for differences when the fabric is gathered or spread flat. An experienced shade-maker will know if it is feasible to use a particular sheer for a shade, and whether it needs lining. Search out other specialists for custom-made shutters, glass bricks, etched glass, and the shiniest of surfaces.

Opposite Natural light defines window shapes and what is beyond, as well as effecting gradations of light and dark within a room. This picture window is left undressed to focus attention on a wonderful vista. It frames a porch lamp, a bird sculpture, and a lush garden. Stone-colored paint highlights the window frame, giving it a strong connection to the modern art gracing the walls.

Above A family living room where adults and children gather informally needs to feel friendly and inviting. If it lacks sunbeams, suggest them with warm tones. The dusky salmon pinks on the walls and touches of corn yellow in the unlined shades make this room vital and welcoming. White covers, a pale floor, and distressed wooden furniture reflect and bounce around the available sunlight.

Below Translucent glass, pure, clean shapes, and pale, bleached tones create the illusion of natural sunshine, even if it is in short supply.

Right A summery, rose-sprigged bedroom is guaranteed to lift the spirits. Yellow is a cheerful and calming color, and layering tone on tone from dense cream to sharp lemon produces a fresh, yet relaxing effect.

Opposite A splash of brilliant natural sunlight gives any room an acute natural advantage.

Radiant Spaces

A blast of sunlight in a big, square room is a tantalizing beginning for a decorating scheme. But if you cast a glance beyond the window, you can use the view as a source of inspirational images that you can then employ inside. This country bedroom overlooks a beautiful flower garden with fields beyond, making the view a visual feast in the summer. Butter yellows with fresh white, a dash of pink, and the curls of opening rosebuds form a natural, irresistible starting point.

Above all, a bedroom needs to be comfortable, but it also needs an intimate atmosphere. It should be a stimulating place to start the day, and a cozy retreat for shutting out the world. If you control the light filtering in, the mood will naturally follow. Awash with sunlight, this room could feel cold because big windows and broad proportions can make a room seem cavernous. Glowing, friendly colors are needed to enhance the sunshine, and individual focuses need to be created to break up the large space: an area for sleeping, one for relaxing, and one for dressing.

A bedroom also needs personality along with a sense of style. Rejecting the received country house or rustic cottage image, the owners wanted something pretty with a

breezy atmosphere. Classic roses from the garden set the scene. Timelessly appealing, they can be as contemporary or retrospective as you wish and, mixed with plain, fresh colors, will create a chic, modern look.

The perfect yellow

Yellow is a notoriously difficult shade to get right, but, once achieved, it is one of the easiest and most glorious colors to live with. It is never out of fashion and is always welcoming, whatever the weather outside. Yet finding that perfect shade can be a struggle. Too much green and it will look sharp, too creamy and it will be insipid, too strong and you will be living with custard. Experimentation is the key, especially in a sunny room. Sunlight tends to bleach out yellows that look strong on paint swatches so paint small patches in different tones on the walls of an empty room and observe the effects over the course of a week.

Where contrasting colors might create a conflict of attention, a combination of yellows, from creamy linen tones to buttercup and lemon, works with the sun to create a flood of color throughout the room. Use translucent textiles and pale surfaces to enhance the light. Poor floorboards can be painted white, but remember that in a bedroom comfort is paramount. Here, a sisal-wool mix ivory carpet reflects light upward and is soft underfoot. Natural weaves are no longer restricted to neutral shades, but are available in a wide spectrum of colors.

Big windows need to be considered carefully so that the flow of light can be controlled. These windows have their original paneling and shutters intact, but what may look elegantly unadorned in a living room will look positively bare in a bedroom. Dress curtains give a more delicate finish, while shutters can be used to screen very bright sunlight and can be closed at night for privacy. Choose a fabric that looks its best unlined: here a loose-weave cream linen gently filters the sun and moves in the breeze of an open window. Plain fabrics are more practical because gentle color and pattern are easily bleached out by the sun.

Left A single fabric design can be used in several guises throughout a room. A classic, rose-print cotton becomes an oilcloth for a kitchen chair seat, seamlessly blending furniture and bed linen. Look, too, for designs reinterpreted on filmy voiles which are perfect for dress curtains in light, bright rooms.

Opposite The open weaves of voile and linen, in single tones, with accents of white, are essential components for a light-enhancing scheme.

Above Little bedroom luxuries—a soft, padded hanger, hand-embroidered linens for mixing and matching, and a spare quilt for chilly nights—add extra nuances of color to the scheme.

Around the four-poster bed voile dress curtains are also filmy and unlined, yet their yellow-and-white stripes show up clearly away from the light source.

A rose-sprigged bed

In a bedroom of plain fabrics, the bed can afford to be indulgently patterned. Just for a change, eschew monastic white bed linen and switch the focus to decadent blossom-strewn designs. A rose-sprigged duvet with dashes of pink and a scattering of white dots sets the tone for a pure and pretty style, and adds all the extra color required as a foil for the buttercup yellows. Look out for bed linens that can be bought with matching fabric. Scatter pillows in the same print help to draw together the bed and sofa area, and a matching oilcloth brightens up an old kitchen chair. Conversely, remember that lots of bedding can also be custom-made and you do not have to rely on ready-made designs. Thick quilted cottons, like this plaid, can be stitched into wonderful bedcovers. This, too, is echoed in the scatter pillow on the sofa. The goal in a bedroom is to create a bed that looks inviting. Good-quality pillows, a plump comforter and a firm mattress are indispensable.

Pure country style

Furniture choices maintain the simple and fresh country style. Unremarkable pieces—a cumbersome armoire, an old kitchen chair, a 1950s-style side table, and a long, narrow sofa—are solid and unassuming, neither too rustic nor too ornate. Reinvented with a wash of white latex and, for the sofa, a loose slipcover in a sheer lemon linen, they are chic in style and provide the perfect contrast to the prettiness of the bed.

Above A twirly wrought-iron bed and feather-light dress curtains insure a sunny, airy feel.

Right A pure and simple style needs the odd glamorous fillip. The beaded pendant adds a sophisticated touch to an otherwise utilitarian armoire, while other light-refracting details, like a crystal droplet hanging from a light pull and a glass bead-encrusted doorknob, add sparkle, too.

Opposite An intimate seating area, with a sofa for lounging on and a side table for easy breakfasts, fills up the vast floor space.

SPACE

Space to stride through, stretch out in, chase the kids across, or party in; corners to snuggle in; vistas from room to room. We all have a natural desire for space in our homes, yet this precious commodity is disappearing fast. Modern homes are frequently small, and grander houses are divided up into apartments. In search of larger living spaces, city dwellers are exploring lofts, converted factories, schools and dockside warehouses. Each presents a unique dilemma. Too little space and we feel claustrophobic; too much and we take fright, fearing a loss of intimacy. With money, time, and commitment you can surely move walls, build up and out, add and take away. But if these are not available to you, artful planning with what you have and skillful illusion can also work wonders.

Left The glory of an open-plan loft is the absence of restrictive internal walls. Yet even the most free-spirited of living quarters needs some way to distinguish areas for different functions such as eating, sleeping, entertaining, and working. It is often better to use color and form than to erect physical partitions. Here, a background of pure white walls and bleached wooden floorboards emphasizes the feeling of space. Skinny blocks of cool navy kitchen cabinets and a contemporary rug define key areas, without overpowering the seamless expanse of the whole.

Opposite In a small studio apartment, a block of solid color on a wall marks out a sleeping area from the rest of the space. Your choice of color is as important as how you use it. A somber navy blue creates a feeling of peace.

SOURCES OF INSPIRATION

The way we live today requires us to re-evaluate our living spaces. We may have extended families, work at home, and prefer flexible, less formal environments.

Generous, meager or plain irregular, a room's proportions exert a fundamental influence. We should not overlook them in the exciting search for pretty fabrics or paint colors. Stand in an empty room considering the needs created by its proportions, and decorating ideas will come to you. Your creative thoughts may not stir until faced with a practical problem. A low-ceilinged, poky spare room or a drafty living room can open your mind to new ideas. An outsize, flower-strewn wallpaper design rejected for the bedroom might be used to distract attention from a difficult space. Replacing two shabby sofas with one huge one will change the spatial proportions of a room.

Make yourself aware of how others use space. Chic, large-scale restaurants, clothing stores, or interior-designed hotels may suggest ideas for lighting, furniture placement, or flower arrangements in bigger spaces, or clever ways to link one room to another. Take photographs; amass pictures from magazines; look at the proportions of furniture; and adapt ideas about storage, which is vital, whatever amount of space you have.

USING SPACE: LARGE ROOMS

A big living area is exhilarating. You get all the benefits of a high ceiling, large windows, and space, even if the one room has to accommodate a variety of activities. If it is a room with a single function, so much the better. Huge rooms give lots of scope for interpretation. You can go for a grand style if architectural detailing allows; experiment with minimalism; show off furniture; display large pieces of art. Decoratively, you can be experimental because unusual patterns or colors will not be in such sharp focus. Yet, great expanses can be cold and drafty; dwarf existing furniture; diminish a carefully chosen pattern; and be very expensive to decorate.

If you want to make the room more intimate, and you like the effects of pattern, strong designs will generally lessen the feeling of space. Tall walls and expansive furniture can take the drama of big, bold stripes, trailing floral bouquets, flying birds,

of space, then work to enhance it. Matte-painted walls in white or cool, bright colors, the contemporary, reflective surfaces of stainless steel or zinc, an expanse of pale marble or bleached oak floor, will all result in a greater feeling of space. Emphasize the height of tall windows with slim, unlined curtain panels on a narrow, high pole, or roll-up shades that retract out of sight during the day.

Big rooms demand bold furniture, so consider selling or swapping key pieces to get the scale right. If that is not an option, consider how to place smaller pieces. Grouping sofas and chairs around one or two coffee tables in the center of the room allows for intimacy, while maintaining a feeling of spaciousness. Plumb a large-scale bath into the middle of a bathroom or even in a big bedroom, and make the connecting bath-room into a dressing room. If it is modern minimalism you are after, have very little furniture, so long as it is quirky or unusual enough to merit the attention it will attract. A few major accessories—a giant gilded mirror, a single large vase with flowers on a grand scale, an outsize floor lamp—will have a greater impact than a host of smaller objects.

USING SPACE : SMALL ROOMS

A room may feel cramped because it was built that way or because it is in a converted property. Smaller spaces have their merits, though; they can be cozy retreats and are easy to keep warm. Moreover, it may be the one room in the house that is your own. They can also be frustratingly difficult to furnish, with a narrow door that excludes furniture, or only enough floor space for a sofa bed. Storage potential will be limited, light may be poor because of small windows, or the proportions

or modern geometrics. The bigger the repeat pattern, the better. Take care to avoid too regular a motif, which on a large scale may realign into irritating diagonals, particularly on wallpaper. But archive designs, originally destined for large houses, may have a more irregular distribution across a large expanse. Unless you want to create a textural effect, steer clear of smaller patterns. Layer patterns in varying scales and designs, not only for a visual feast but also because they will give the illusion of intimacy. Textured draperies; broad valances, cornices, or lambrequins; chunky curtain poles; and the use of pattern will bring down the height of large windows.

The judicious use of strong, bright, or warm colors will prevent a cavernous feel. If, on the other hand, you have bought your loft apartment specifically because you love the feeling

may be odd. Reduce frustration by thinking how a room is to be used. If a kitchen is big enough to include a dining area, it is far better to reinvent the dining room as a study than to struggle with furniture that simply will not fit.

Turn problems to your advantage. Lots of detail in a small room can distract the eye from tiny proportions and trick it into thinking everything is much grander. You can indulge in small-scale prints, weaves, and needlepoint fabrics because they will be seen up close and be on smaller pieces of furniture. Texture, too, takes on fresh significance. Try tactile wool, suede, or brushed cotton on chairs or draperies, with pillows and throws in something silkier for contrast. If the room is to be a retreat, choose deep, warm colors to enhance the mood and cram in lots of pictures, books, and favorite things.

Opposite A vast wall mirror never fails visually to push back the walls of a small room. The illusion of space is further enhanced by using a subtle monochrome palette, simple block shapes, and minimal accessories.

Above Decorating an enormous room requires careful planning and furniture that is in proportion. Small furniture would look insignificant. Such a room needs stretched sofas, outsize tables, and massive cabinets. The towering windows in this living room are brought down to human scale by half-lowering the shades. Similarly, artifacts are hung midway up the wall.

If you need to push back the walls visually in a main living space, choose colors in pale, matte shades; ruthlessly cut down on furniture; and keep accessories to a minimum. Try tricks, such as vertically striped walls, to make the ceiling seem higher; or remove central pendant light fixtures and keep floors pale and reflective. Floor-to-ceiling cabinets with unadorned doors, painted to blend in with the walls, form the least obtrusive storage. Use alcoves or the space above a door for cup-boards or shelves. Keep the floor space as empty as possible. Trim beds and sofas with long skirts to conceal storage space.

LINKING SPACES

Every house has its own configuration of linking spaces that offer an extra decorating dimension. When planning a new scheme, consider the colors of your hallway and stair-case or, even better, change them too. Play with unity or unexpected contrasts. Choose a main fabric color from the living room and use it in the hallway to unify the two spaces. Or use one of your accent colors in the hallway for a surprising yet cohesive contrast. Have a fresh look at coordinated fabric collections that include stripes and checks with a large- and smaller-scale main pattern. Use one combination in the principal room, and another in the adjoining room to create a subtle change of tone.

The view from one room to the next is invariably framed by a doorway. You might remove the door and paint the trim a different color to highlight the effect. Exploit the area beyond to create a deliberate tableau with a curvy item of furniture, a favorite picture, or a display of flowers.

DEFINING SPACE

Large kitchens that have enough space for eating, working, and socializing are today often the heart of a house and take precedence over formal living rooms. The blurring of physical

Left A pitched ceiling, out-of-kilter walls, or any unusually proportioned space requires thought. The sloping roof beam could have dominated this small room. Instead, it is a characterful feature in a dining area where ceiling height is not so vital.

Below In a modern kitchen where light is essential and through traffic inevitable, a light-refracting screen supported on elegant struts is ideal to define the work space. Planned with an eye for proportion and detail, a screen is a thing of beauty, too.

Left A substantial piece of furniture can work in a small room if the space surrounding it remains uncluttered. Four-poster beds are most often found in grand interiors, but this light and elegant design looks intimate and inviting in a room where the yellow ocher walls have been left deliberately unadorned. The filmy bed drapes diffuse and soften the light as it passes through.

boundaries within a home means that more people live, work, and play within single, larger spaces. You may want to consider ways of defining open-plan areas, so that everyone is clear where they can be busy and where they should be calm. You could use different colors to designate spatial boundaries, for example. Create an abstract pattern as a decorative dividing line across a floor. Or the sunny side of an apartment might be devoted to areas of daytime activity, and the darker side reserved for after-dark entertaining, bathing (plumbing permitting), and sleeping.

If you prefer or need physical divisions, install large wooden dividing doors across a living room to create a social space and a work or play area. Or run a curtain pole across at ceiling height. Experiment with roll-up shades as partitions. Contemporary spaces might call for sliding doors or large screens on wheels. With these physical boundaries, you may want to keep the adjoining spaces in style.

115

Minimal Dimensions

Strictures on space necessitate inventive solutions. Small and dark, with the worst of views, a tiny room reinvents itself in a fresh new guise. In the scramble for space, a home office can be created out of the humblest of dimensions, yet it can still offer imaginative surprises. Lack of space calls for restraint, organization, and punctilious order. Here, the soothing colors of indigo and taupe, sourced from balls of string, provide the parameters for an oasis of calm.

A small store room presents myriad problems. Dimensions may seem hopelessly unworkable, light may be scanty, and atmosphere may be nonexistent. Empty and unloved, and measuring 7 ft. 6 in. x 8 ft. 3 in. (2 m x 2.5 m),

this tiny room looked so small that the thought of furnishing it seemed daunting. The room is also north-facing, with gloomy shadows and a cool air. However, it still has potential. A tape measure, run along the walls and around potential furniture, establishes that there is room for basics—so long as you apply judicious forethought. The generous window provides the focus on one wall and supplies plenty of light for a study area. At the same time, that diffuse and shady light prompts a rethink in mood. After all, a study needs to be soothing and composed. Teamed with underwater colors and gently glinting surfaces, shady light can be turned into an advantage, generating a studious atmosphere and a crisp and workmanlike style.

Above The oatmeal hues of string, the creamy beige of a manila envelope, or the pastel colors of a postage stamp can provide a multitude of color inspirations.

Left The luxury of having a separate home office makes the tiniest of rooms look appealing.

Opposite Rigorous planning of equipment is vital in a home office: the computer terminal, printer, fax, telephone, and answering machine all need to be accessible, with cords tucked well out of the way.

Small-scale planning

A sliver of workable space is only as useful as its capacity for storage, which needs to be planned with rigorous precision. In a home office, more than any other room, efficiency is paramount. The basics—a desk, a back-supporting chair, storage for papers, and other paraphernalia—need to be sorted out first. Then, if there is any remaining space, you can think about introducing additions such as an armchair for relaxed reading. Think practically about cabinets. There might not be enough room to open and close doors, making open shelving preferable. In order to take up minimal floor space, stack storage into a tall, narrow structure. In this particular room, conventional office equipment is jettisoned in favor of more unusual pieces: a Gustavian-style table doubles as a desk and a slim, galvanized-steel drawer unit holds the bulk of home office filing.

The shape, finish, and placement of furniture in a room will inevitably have an impact on the space. Be aware of this and look for themes to highlight. The almond-colored wood and silvery steel of the desk and drawer unit create an

Above Rules are relaxed in a home office. A radio for catching the lunchtime news, flowers on the desk, and the indulgence of ink instead of ballpoint pens are enticing extras.

Right An understated mix of plain linens and a businesslike ticking makes for a calming, tailored scheme centered around blues and neutrals. Investing time to decorate a home office properly pays dividends: it feels like a proper work space and makes it a pleasurable place to be.

Opposite Even the smallest of spaces can be stretched to accommodate a working area and a relaxing corner. Counteract the harsh angles of technology with a curvy chair, a floppy pillow and an unstructured laundry bag for magazines and books. A picture on the wall in place of a calendar or clock promotes a cozier ambience.

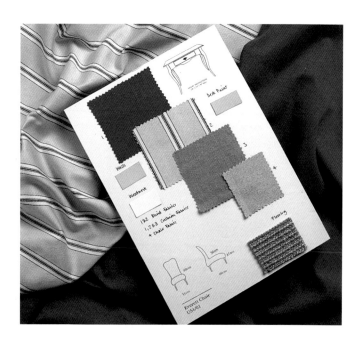

Right Utilize spare wall space for individual storage boxes, so that pencils, postcards, notepads, and string are easily at hand.

Below The ubiquitous office bulletin board gets a revamp. A silvery memo board is practical, yet when stuck with favorite art postcards it looks beautiful, too.

Window treatments in small rooms are just as important as those in larger ones. In an office, some form of screen is essential, especially if a workstation is to be situated near direct sunlight, which may need to be blocked out. However, curtains take up precious wall space and reduce the amount of light in dark rooms. A shade, conversely, can be rolled up out of the way. Instead of the more utilitarian roll-up shade, a Roman shade has been chosen, as its pleated folds and contrasting edging soften the hard angles of office equipment, creating a gentler environment. A vertical ticking stripe creates the illusion of height. With a touch of irony, its shirty stripes are a visual reference to the conventions of an office world left far behind.

initial visual tension between grainy and shiny surfaces; on a broader plane, this can be seen as a juxtaposition between antique lines and contemporary styling, which sets a pattern for the rest of the room. The blond-wood shelf unit contrasts with the creamy brushstrokes on the traditional drawer chest; tubular steel and pale ply meet in the swivel chair; and accessories also take up the theme.

A tranquil palette

A tiny space will need to be extended visually: the ceiling needs to be pushed up, and the walls forced back. Colors and patterns can be either beneficial or intrusive, so they should be chosen with care. In its new role as a home office, this small room also needs a calm, soothing palette. Blue is a natural choice for a working environment; it is associated with restful thought and, provided the right shade is chosen, it is cooling rather than cold. A true, ocean aqua—opt for paint rather than fussier wallpaper—revitalizes the dull walls and provides a plain, serene backdrop to counteract the inevitable clutter of office equipment and stationery. Crisp white paintwork emphasizes the window, and insures that it remains a central feature in the room.

Restricted space works better with a restricted palette, and fabric choices should reflect the tones already established in a room scheme. Here a cozy armchair smartens up in neutral linen, and a hyacinth blue fabric graces the office chair. No-nonsense sisal matting on the floor is similarly neutral, maximizing the available floor space.

Classic meets contemporary

A principal delight of the home office is that it can be full of the latest technology, yet it still remains infinitely more welcoming than an office at work. Office chairs can be covered in linen and storage boxes in flower-strewn wallpaper.

Accessorizing becomes more fun when everyday objects—a raffia basket, a fabric laundry bag—can be turned into storage facilities, and when the luxury of comfort raises the tone.

The accessories in this office take up the classic and contemporary themes: a retro silver lamp hovers over a state-of-the-art computer terminal; metal tea tins and linen-covered disk files contrast with acrylic and chrome boxes; the bulletin board is hi-tech chrome, while the pictures are framed art photographs. Together, they provide a visual feast. Yet, essential to small-space living, these same items are carefully arranged on the shelves to promote unity of line, and the illusion of order. In tiny rooms, the visual tricks really do count.

ARCHITECTURAL DETAIL

Sometimes grand, often rather modest, there are some rooms that positively shout for attention. They are so beautifully constructed that they simply cannot be ignored. A generous ceiling molding, lofty floor-to-ceiling double-hung windows or glazed doors, a gently curved wall or arched doorway, or an intricately tiled fireplace—all such features capture our gaze and please our senses. Period architecture is crammed with special details; you may not love them all but any sensitive decorator will work with and around them. You may admire windows for their symmetry, and coves for their intricacy or enjoy the way time has worn and molded floors, bent door frames, cracked and added character to original plaster walls. But re-evaluate, too, what features modern buildings have to offer.

Above Modern features in a classically proportioned room can look beautiful as well as radical. Here, the gentle scroll of ironwork on the balcony and the ornate cove detailing are appreciated afresh when seen in contrast to the clean-cut lines of a modern fireplace and contemporary furniture. A white palette unifies the period and modern styles.

Opposite Whether a house is grand or humble, cultivate the art of faking architectural detail where none exists. Many houses lack character because original features have been removed or were in short supply at the time of building. A confident strip of navy at the base of saffron yellow walls gives definition to this cottage interior. Consider how to make the most of vistas framed by open doors.

SOURCES OF INSPIRATION

Most of us recognize the importance of preserving original architectural features, but, after the craze for Victoriana, modernism again beckons. Rather than seeking to restore authentically, we tend to use individual period features to inspire and direct us. Mosaic floor tiles in a grand old house may suggest a modern use of somber, chalky shades; or double-hung windows with original shutters may become part of a contemporary, less-is-more interior. Scour your interior for architectural details that might inspire a fresh idea. But do not look at a room in isolation, because detailing is likely to recur in slight variations throughout the house.

Consider the proportions and major features of a room: the doors, windows, floor, and fireplace. Windows dominate, so their style is likely to set a decorative tone. Look at textures and shades. Do dark floorboards inspire a play of chocolate and cream neutrals? A gray marble fireplace might suggest a combination of cool surfaces. Is there a plaster frieze, a fireplace tile? What motifs do they contain? An abstract swirl or some tiny birds or delicate roses could set off a theme. If intricate plasterwork has lost its definition under many layers of paint, work back to the original.

If inspiration lies in the physical shape and presence of one feature, most likely a dramatic fireplace or unusually shaped window, devise a scheme to throw attention onto it. If rooms lack detail, search through catalogs of fireplaces, moldings, and tiles, and books on architectural detailing and the history of interior design. Visit architectural salvage yards and search through builders' rubble; you never know what you might find. But if blue-and-white Delft tiles inspire you to impose a complete Dutch-parlor period look, exercise a little restraint. A looser interpretation might be less time-consuming and more creative.

USING EXISTING FEATURES

In a house blessed with original features, such as wall paneling or slim eighteenth-century windows with inset seats and wooden shutters, it is tempting to decorate in period style with authentic paint colors and finishes, appropriate furniture, and archive fabric designs. But remember that your home is not a museum; it is somewhere for you to live and enjoy. Attempt such a recreation with humor and a light touch so that you interpret a period feel and capture a mood. Certain architectural features call

not for a period interpretation but, rather, for a general empathy. An old house or country cottage with wide, worn floorboards and bumpy plaster can cry out for traditional paints in dusky shades—yet modern upholstery and curtain treatments in crisp, functional fabrics would look more upbeat than the customary florals and patchwork quilts.

Treat elegant period details such as old wood floors, tall windows, or grand fireplaces as simply as possible, rather than detracting from them with fussy curtains or grand mirrors. Mix them with contemporary pieces of furniture or brightly

colored walls. Such unexpected combinations create drama, surprise, and a new focus. Or try setting a period sofa against the whitewashed brick wall of a converted warehouse.

If a floor tile or perhaps a stained-glass window has a significant design or motif, adapt it to create a room scheme. An organic design, such as a leaf or an apple, could be echoed in patterned textiles—or on other hard surfaces in the room. For example, if you wanted a new radiator cover you could trace the original motif, photocopy it up to the right proportions, and have it cut out of the cover. Bold-scale stenciling still has a place in some decorative schemes, so use your pattern to hand-cut a stencil. If your inspiration stems from a more abstract pattern, such as a carved trellis design, consider repeating it as a painted or stenciled design on the floor, as part of a built-in shelf detail, or sandblasted onto glass.

Architectural features can act as decorative *objets d'art*. A weathered arched window frame could simply be propped against a wall or secured above a fireplace, or a piece of detailed molding hung as a picture. Similar finds would be fun seen emerging from a cluster of leafy indoor plants.

ADDING FEATURES

Architectural features shape and define a room; without them a space may appear bare and impersonal. They can be added, whether it is molded plasterwork or a different kind of door, or faked. Although making changes stylistically can create wonderful surprises, a room with a mix of grand Swedish Gustavian paneling and enormous old-fashioned radiators might look rather odd. Visit houses similar to yours; you may find one that still has original features that could guide you. And do not forget to balance scale.

If doors and windows have been replaced with modern aluminum frames, or they lack paneling, a primary concern will be to revert to original styles. It is better to spend money on getting the bare bones right, and choose a less expensive decorating scheme. And classic, chunky central heating radiators do look much nicer than trim modern ones. Authentic is not always best, however. In a cool, contemporary sitting room it might be better visually to swap an original heavy black fireplace for a curvier marble French-style one, despite a cross-over of styles. If you add detailed coves for grandeur, it does not mean you have to have chair rails, too.

As decorating looks are simpler nowadays, add details only to create definition rather than as extraneous clutter. Too many modern or converted properties are given thin, meager-looking baseboards, whereas a generous 10 in. (23 cm) board with a complex molding adds enriching detail and a solid base to a room. To change the look of a room radically, consider full or partial paneling created by a specialist carpenter, or ready-made paneling designed to slot together.

So that added features do not look new or fake, blend them in by using as many original materials as possible. Have a carpenter rework beautiful, discarded wood paneling as molding around a door or window. When the real thing is not available, try visual tricks. Paint new wooden shutters or baseboards and gently distress them to match a painted antique

in the room. Highlight and slightly age moldings by adding a faint line of a darker shade of paint or a subtle hint of broken gilding. Moldings look more authentic if they are painted in a mix of muted neutrals rather than pristine white.

Architectural definition can be hinted at with paint, if it is used cleverly. A bold line of color can trick the eye. If there is no molding but the ceiling is high, consider painting the ceiling in a deep shade, taking the color down as far as an imaginary cove. Likewise, a painted strip at the base of a wall will suggest a baseboard. Broad strips of color around windows and doors without moldings will help to define them. Or colored tiles could be used in place of the painted strip. Although you need a lot of confidence to create false paneling on walls, perhaps by

Opposite Decorative ironwork can be a rich source of inspiration. The intricately curved bases of this period banister have become a design template. It is not slavishly copied, but subtly interpreted in the entry hall below it: in a loose swirl on the border of the carpet, in the organic curve of a velvety chaise longue, and in the curvaceous legs of the table.

Above This mad mix of different architectural styles gathered together in one room might have been a disaster. The ornate mantel, solidly simple fireplace, and tongue-and-groove wall paneling in this informal living room hail from very different eras. But when they are all painted white, one's attention is directed, instead, to the family's favorite treasures—an oil painting, an antique textile, a child's chair.

glazed cabinets. Imagine a soft tangerine backdrop to blue-and-white china, or gray behind cranberry-colored glasses.

THE PRACTICALITIES

As a purist, you will want to restore precious details, stick to authentic materials, and hover around the historically correct boundaries. But the cost of restoring a feature may far outweigh the price of replacing it with something almost identical; and the use of an authentic paint finish may not be practical for late twentieth-century living. Putting in an authentic plaster molding may give you pleasure, but once it is painted, it will look much the same as a cheaper resin one. But beware. Some are clumsily drawn, so scrutinize cheaper resin or wood moldings and detailing for their quality of design. They will often look cheap no matter how you paint them. The same goes for reproduction fireplaces. Prices vary enormously between styles but choose the best one you can afford as it will be a major focal point.

copying a pattern from a book or magazine of historical interiors, the results can be utterly convincing, as can painting fake tiles onto floors or walls.

Traditionally, white or a pale neutral is used for ceilings and woodwork, but it is fun to use color for moldings, around doors, or on wooden floors. It does not have to be a strongly contrasting color, simply a slightly paler shade of that on the walls, or one of the colors in the wallpaper. Using color like this highlights lovely architectural detailing; adds emphasis if the moldings are not spectacular; and lends confidence and cohesion to a decorative scheme. To draw instant attention to displays, try painting the interiors of built-in shelves or

Armed with your design, and having decided how you are going to put it all together, and the quality you are hoping to achieve, the last stage, as always, is to find specialist sources. Look at catalogs to consider both cheap options and com-panies specializing in faithful period copies, traditional materials, and modern versions. Search out architectural salvage yards and, importantly, a creative carpenter to adapt your finds sympathetically. Gather historically correct paint charts and discuss your needs with paint specialists. They are a mine of information and most are quite used to mixing a special color to match the minutest chip of original paint.

Opposite Updated cream paneling and simple styling in this bedroom successfully combine modernity with respect for the original features.

Left Have no qualms about faking architectural features. Paneling is one of the easiest effects to try. Ready-made moldings are simply glued to the wall, and when painted look just as elegant as the real thing.

Above The bold rectangular shapes of the contemporary furniture blend easily with the simple geometric design of the paneling in this period interior. Just as easily, the herringbone patterns of the polished wood floor might have inspired the use of textiles with related textures or patterns.

A Dominant Fireplace

A fireplace is a centralizing feature. By day, it forms a natural decorative focus, dominating a room with its color nuances: the cool grays of marble or the soft, biscuity tones of stone. At night, full of blazing logs, it holds a room in thrall, creating an intimate and relaxed atmosphere. But no fireplace is perfect. This one is dark and imposing and tends to overwhelm the room. It needs a bold decorating hand to restore equilibrium to the living room.

There is a subtle difference between balancing the weight of a dominant feature in the context of a room—which is a positive exercise—and trying to camouflage it. In this room, the fireplace is a glorious celebration of the Victorian era: heavy slate, marble panel and intricate, decorative tiles. The issue is not whether the fireplace looks good, but whether the black, salmon, and parchment color scheme are out of step in a family living room. For a space that needs to be vital and stimulating, working a scheme around its prevailing dark tones is not a sensible option.

The answer lies in a confident decorative approach. Bold, daring patterns and large, chunky furniture with a strong personality will move attention away from the fireplace and around the room. A striking apple green, just glimpsed among the fireplace tiles, forms the seed of an idea for a vivacious, contemporary revamp.

Above A fireplace can be multi-faceted. Examine it for themes to be drawn out, specks of color awaiting discovery, or textural hints within rough-hewn stone or stately marble.

Left and Opposite The generous proportions of a wide bay window and the gift of day-long sunshine are not enough to counteract a heavy, dark fireplace. However, color-drenched walls and the confident mixing of abstract patterns turn an unexceptional room into a comfortable, vibrant family living room.

Right Large-scale pattern repeats call for careful planning. Start off with a standard-size colorboard and amass the different shades and companion fabrics, then bring home show-length pieces of material to try out in the room itself.

Above Highlight a single motif from an abstract or pictorial pattern in a panel on a pillow. A border in a toning or contrasting textile, with or without welting, will give the design a fresh slant. Intersperse heavily patterned pillows with simply tailored plain pillows, featuring self-buttoning, pintucks, or ties.

Shifting the focus

There are some large-scale, abstract motifs that cannot help but distract and it is these that form the nucleus of the room's new look. Large-scale patterns call for strong, vibrant walls to maintain equilibrium. You may think that this room, with its lofty ceiling and generous bay window, provides the perfect space for experimenting with samples of wild, wacky wallpaper, but this would only fight with the fireplace rather than playing it down. Instead, apple green instantly tempers the dark hues of the fireplace and adds vibrancy and modernity to the room.

For the windows, a crisp cotton sporting a stylized daisy in dènim blue and honey hangs as draperies, a wide, navy border

Opposite Here picture and print choices have been left until last. Their variegated tones are used to draw out particular shades in the scheme. A plain linen mount or handpainted frame could also be chosen to echo a vivid accent shade.

around the leading edge drawing your attention. Roman shades in a pencil-thin denim stripe add to the effect. In addition, a madras check in denim blue and apple green covers the sofa which, placed opposite the fireplace, serves to balance it.

Once started, the mixture of patterns gathers momentum. The bolder the mix of designs, the more they seem to call for additional patterns to give them a third dimension. Tiny checks are natural mixers, as are stripes or abstract prints. However, any further pattern on the armchairs might be unsettling, so deeper blues, running to indigo and navy, define their shape as well as being more appropriate near the dark hearth.

Where patterns compete, use unifying strands to link the elements. In this room, the pillows create that unity. Each one is unique, yet each one is also a reflection of another textile in the room. A single daisy forms a central panel, the pencil stripe a broad border, while the apple-colored linen and unbroken madras check are used for contrasting welting. Using the remnants from draperies, shades, and covers is a foolproof way of anchoring an entire scheme and reiterating its themes.

Flooring should not be an afterthought in a busy scheme. It needs to be considered and matched with key textiles. A living room needs flooring that is comfortable and durable, yet smart and attractive. Where dark floorboards may have muddied the other colors, a tightly knit honey sisal gives a clean finish.

Opposite A stunning fireplace deserves to be dressed up. Draw attention to it with candles, scented or otherwise, for atmosphere, with piled-up logs and a fireside chair close by. Try to keep the traditional mantelpiece clutter of invitations, letters, and keys at bay.

Above Weave grown-up detailing into a family-centered room. A gilded candelabra comes into its own by night.

Right Make accessories work. Matte cream and spun gold plant pots reflect the contrast of cream-painted wooden furniture and elaborate gilded detailing.

Defining the fireplace

However beautiful its composition, or curvaceous its lines, a fireplace may need a little help to fulfill its potential. Pay attention to what it is doing in the room. If the fireplace is to be used at night for a spectacular real fire, the hearth can be piled high with logs, while coals are kept in a basket alongside gleaming fire tools and a guard. If the fireplace is a purely decorative feature, perhaps a delicate needlepoint firescreen is all that is needed to set it off. What goes above the fireplace, and what is arranged on the mantelpiece, is important, too.

The dense materials of this fireplace, heavy slate and marble, need to be offset by lighter touches. A mirror is essential for maximizing light and counteracting the dark mantelpiece, and its thick, golden frame works just as well with the clear, fresh green of the walls as with the dark tones below. Gilded and elaborately branched candelabra set with creamy candles are pretty by day and glint in the mirror at night, transforming a family room into an atmospheric drawing room. The wall-mounted candelabra add still more sparkle and shine.

A Decorative Entrance

A period house is crammed with patterns cut into glass, carved into wood, or traced within ironwork. An entry is as good a starting point as any. Look to the colors and designs of original floor tiles for inspiration, and upward to a fanlight of wonderful colored glass. The fretwork detailing of this hallway arch resembles a Caribbean beach house, prompting the choice of soft, ice-cream colors for an upbeat start.

Above The intricate lines of a finely wrought motif or the twist of a rail may contain the kernel of a decorative idea.

Right From a standard, narrow high-traffic area to one with its own charm, this turn-of-the-century entry hall gets a radical facelift.

Opposite The Caribbean flavor of the original archway inspires a dreamy eau-de-Nil and aqua scheme, which harmonizes with the tiled floor.

An entry hall is the gateway to the rest of the house. It is where we say hello and goodbye, linger for a chat, hurry up and down stairs, deposit bags, and open mail. It is a high-traffic area, most likely to have its floors soiled with mud and its walls scraped with buggies. For all these reasons, it should be planned as a light and uplifting place, practical enough to withstand all this action while exuding a warm and welcoming ambience.

This entry benefits from being sunny and wide. It has a pair of attractive double doors and the archway creates a natural visual pause before the passageway and stairs beyond. Dense, creamy color forms part of the plan, but so too does the pursuit of that all-important atmosphere.

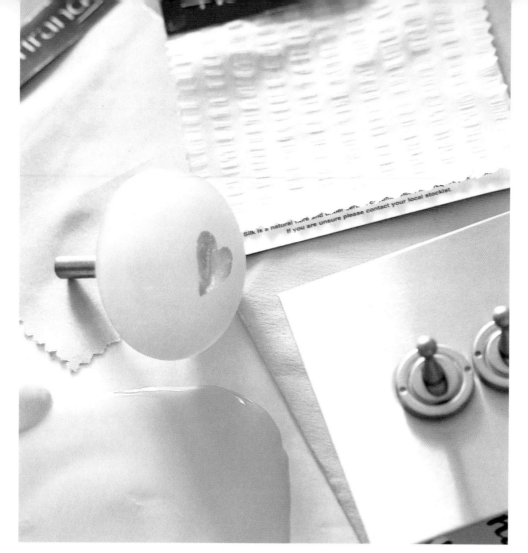

Left and Above A sandblasted doorknob, an ornate letter rack, and the sheen of a chrome light switch provide the finishing touches.

Opposite The gently curved base of these shades echoes the sweeping curves of the door and those of the decorative archway.

Stamping a personality

However intricate its detailing, however sunny its aspect, an entry is generally a cold and drafty place, with a hard floor underfoot and no furniture to lend it charm. It is for this reason that the spectrum of Caribbean shades—marshmallow pink, lemon yellow, leaf green, sea aqua, and blue—is so tempting. Although they are all refreshing, light-refracting colors, the aqua shade works best here.

The color scheme in a foyer is as important for the rooms leading off it as it is for the space itself. If you select a shade that is too definite, it will jar with the color scheme of adjoining rooms. Aqua sits happily with white, neutrals, and similarly toned colors, and it also fits in well with the chalky blue, sand, and terra-cotta tiles underfoot. Suggestive of sunny skies and warmth, aqua captures the light and chases away the cold.

An entryhall also needs furniture to give it personality, form, and atmosphere. This is not an impossibility: the narrowest of passageways may have a radiator that can be transformed with a slim decorative cover. Wall-mounted hooks will suffice where a cabinet will not fit. This hallway is wide enough to take a tall, antique hall stand, which easily accommodates the mail, keys, and bags below, and its quirky detailing adds character. A Swedish console, with fretwork around the sides, echoes the fretwork of the decorative arch and turns a passageway into a telephone area.

Textures do not often come to mind when you think of a typical entry hall. Painted walls and flooring are usually the sum total. Yet the contrasts of rough and smooth, shiny and matte, are powerful mood creators. Here, the smoothness of the original tiles is contrasted with the practical, tough weave of the jute herringbone carpet on the stairs; the bumpy detail

of embossed wallpaper is set against the pebble-smooth glass of a door handle traced in silver. It is rare to find textiles in an entry, but they are very good for softening empty spaces. Left unadorned, these glass doors might seem too open, admitting not only bright light, but cold drafts and prying eyes, too. Narrow roll-up shades in silky seersucker with a satin trim prettify and filter the sunlight. Their surprise factor has as much impact as their soft and subtle texture.

A repeated image

An architectural feature with a dominant motif—a leaf that can be copied, a swirl that can be reinterpreted—should be exploited to the full. The carefree loops and clover-leaf shapes found in the archway are drawn onto a radiator cover and cut out; this not only continues the pattern theme but provides essential ventilation too. The swooping tendrils from the archway are also echoed in the curly metal chandelier dangling by the porch.

Above Rooms are often decorated with flowers, and a hall space should be no exception. Consider both color and scent. A bunch of flowers can create a welcoming, perfumed threshold.

Opposite Connecting spaces, like narrow entries and hallways, are frequently neglected in favor of the rooms that open from them. To reverse that trend, make use of flowers and pictures, or artfully arranged *objet d'art*, to create a tableau that can just be glimpsed from the front door—a promise of color and style to come.

Right A radiator cover can be customized to capitalize on a distinctive motif or an architectural feature. Keep the look abstract, or copy it exactly, but do so with a spirit of improvisation and a lightness of touch. These turn-of-the-century swirls and clover leaves take on a contemporary look when transposed as cut-outs for a radiator cover.

TRAVEL

Travel provokes a fresh perspective, bringing with it new inspiration and throwing the familiar elements of our life sharply into focus. Journeying abroad imprints fresh images on our

minds—exhilarating, jumbled, colorful—and enables us to bring new experiences to bear on our normal environment. Little wonder that designers travel the globe seeking new influences in far-flung places, distilling what they see into a new trend. Try to do the same. It might be visual memories that inspire—the dark, bitter colors and rough textures of tribal handicrafts seen in a market, a fleeting glimpse of hot sun on a colorwashed wall—or a treasured item, loved and brought home. Atmosphere plays a part, too: the serenity of a cool, painted church; the relaxing flutter of a curtain at a beach-house window.

SOURCES OF INSPIRATION

Any one influence from abroad could be interpreted in a decorative scheme, but it is always necessary to learn to explore and anchor them in practical terms, adapting foreign styles to your own interior.

It is a rare traveler who returns home without a few treasures, and an even rarer one who does not throw most of them away. Mistakes happen because we do not focus sufficiently on what we might do with a tribal textile or handpainted pot once we are back home. Yet there are always beautiful, stimulating souvenirs that can not only be integrated into our houses, but also be used as a source of inspiration. So shop a little more judiciously, keeping in mind how your home looks. Textiles, such as Thai silks in myriad colors or striped Greek mattress ticking, are very likely to hold their appeal once home, and could play a major part in a scheme, whereas a handstitched Indian pillow cover is more likely destined to be an accessory. You may be inspired by a piece or style of furniture, perhaps a Peruvian carved bench, but think hard before you ship one home. It is amazing how seeing lots of a particular

thing while you are abroad makes you think you just cannot do without one. Far better to take a photograph, consider it, and if you still like it once you are home, look for something similar.

Every region and country has its own distinctive decorative style that will provoke new ideas. Whether you are actually traveling or simply looking through books on foreign interiors, analyze the details of the things that attract you. Is it the style of furniture, unusual paint colors and combinations, or the different textures common to other climates? When you have defined the appeal, you can then select appropriate details for your own scheme. Do not attempt to copy an entire look; go instead for your own unique interpretation of it. The natural light, architectural styles, and particular atmospheres born of cultural variations simply will not translate verbatim to another country.

When you travel, attempt to assimilate the more abstract nuances of atmosphere, image, color, and light that surround you. You do not have to be in far-flung

Opposite, above Pale silvery tongue-and-groove paneling and rustic gingham-edged curtains have their origins in an Alpine retreat or lakeside log cabin. A simple stone sink, abstract pictures, wood detailing, and brick floor all help to make this a warmly welcoming bathroom.

Right The indigenous style of a piece of furniture—even a textile bed-spread—may hint at a country visited and remembered. In this bedroom, the dark wooden chairs, the artfully arranged bamboo, and yellow Chinese panels in the bathroom screen discreetly suggest an Oriental mood.

Opposite, below Grand palaces and churches, ethnic houses and shrines, all steeped in their own culture and decorative style, are imprinted on our memory as we travel. This bedroom's faded tones evoke centuries-old plaster and give it a romantic mood that is further enhanced by well-chosen furniture. An eighteenth-century French Bergère bed, rumpled bed linen and stone corbel nightstands all help to conjure up European elegance at its finest.

Left This intriguing room takes elements from around the world. There are colonial chairs, an ikat cushion, kilim rugs, a tooled-leather box, and tribal pots. The creative mix works because the deliberately neutral walls provide a blank canvas.

Opposite Sizzling and intense colors, seen abroad and adapted for use at home with appropriate textures, are lavishly cheerful and warm. A heady mix of tangerine walls and amethyst paintwork, tribal paintings and an explosion of rich textures and patterns, makes this room lusciously welcoming and unforgettable.

places to glean valuable inspiration, but your responses may be fresher to unfamiliar and perhaps more dramatic regions. A turquoise sky hovering over the sandy wastes of African scrubland may inspire you to put together blues and browns you would never have considered before. The bright light on a February day in New York, combined with urban textures and the steely blue of the sky, might provoke a subtler scheme. As you travel, use your camera, your memory, a sketchbook, or a diary to capture these influences in much the same way as a writer or artist might keep notes for future works.

TRAVEL INFLUENCES

Tapping into foreign influences and styles is a skill in itself. Adapting and anchoring some of them into your overall scheme is more complex. If the hues of a piece of fabric or a unique piece of furniture attract you, then follow the principles set out in earlier chapters for putting a scheme together. But analyzing the appeal of texture, surface, and color variations to see what inspires us is vital, as is picking out cultural and native stylistic differences. Only when we can do this can we begin to copy or adapt the effects to re-create their mood or define a new style.

When you travel you cannot fail to notice the effects of color; its intensity in Mediterranean countries, or along the California coast, or the slightly chalkier pastels daubed throughout the Caribbean. They are seen inside and outside buildings, bursting forth from textiles, and painted on pots. They are there because they work with bright, hot sunshine, and are in tune with the surreal vividness of native fruits, flowers, and vegetables. That is why, if you live in colder climes, it is unwise to adopt them unmodified in your home, no matter how much you love them. In cool northern light, they lose much of their bite and appeal. Instead, pick one or two shades—lemon sherbet or Mediterranean blue, say—and reinterpret them in fabrics, perhaps strong cotton or linen, rather than as overpowering wall colors. Mix in neutrals as a link with your less-than-brilliant light and perhaps more somber natural surroundings, and the adaptation will work.

Then there is texture. Buildings in hot countries are crammed with ceramic tiles, marble, mosaics, and tinted plaster. For those in more northerly climates, the allure lies in their contrast to the materials used at home—wool carpet, tapestry, thick cotton, matte paint or paper on walls. They also appeal because they remind us of atmospheres, the sudden contrast between heat outside and the welcome coolness and smoothness of the textures within. However, skillful adaptation is important. If you cannot live without the brilliance of blue Moroccan mosaic tiles, do not use them on every surface; the final effect could be cold and clinical. Try them as detailing on a kitchen shelf or in patterns on a bathroom floor, and match their intense color with others in softer textures—vivid red towels, perhaps, or a simple shade. Similarly, a southern traveler in northern climes may fall in love with a heavy pure wool carpet but would be unwise to use it at home for anything more than a bedside rug. Some surfaces, such as

the warm tones of Italian palazzo walls, do translate more readily to cooler countries and their architecture. However, think carefully about other styles to match with them. A casual mix of white linen slipcovers or more formal ruched silk draperies may look good individually and feel more natural than using only authentic Italian furniture. A sudden passion for large-scale stone blocks may have been inspired by a visit to a European city palace. A paint-effect wallpaper will recreate such a look, but use it with a sense of humor, and paper somewhere unexpected, like a bathroom.

Window and fabric treatments are directly affected by the rise and fall of temperature which, of course, varies from one country to the next. Take stylistic details from the Greeks, who might hang an unlined fabric panel to float in whatever breeze there is at a window or door. Observe the

way the French often opt for narrow dress curtains pulled aside with tiebacks to leave a plain shade screening the sun. Look at the motifs cut out of the thick wooden shutters on Austrian chalets or the gathered gingham valances teamed with thin voile curtains so beloved of the Swedes. Whether you are in a chic hotel or a stately home abroad, take note of any differences in the way that the beds are dressed, from canopies to sheets. Are pillow covers in unusual styles and shapes? Do they use conventional tablecloths or go for long, thin runners? Observe, too, how patterns and textiles are used in foreign countries. Staying in a French château might just inspire you to try a classic combination of antique toile de Jouy with fresh checks. You might adopt a single batik print seen in Indonesia, reworked as pillows on a plain sofa at home.

Inevitably, there will be souvenirs—lamps, rugs, pictures, ceramics—that are not destined to be interpreted, but can be worked into your scheme to remind you of a happy trip. You can adapt these things, too. If a Madonna image from Spain looks overly gaudy in its gilded frame, reframe it in dark wood. Embroidered white sheets from Hong Kong would look cozier mixed with a rustic blanket. Those too-bright Indian saris you intended for curtains can be cut up and inserted as panels in plainer pillow covers. Edit and adapt, and do not be afraid to lose a "find" that does not fit in.

MODERN TRAVEL INFLUENCES

When we travel, it is the rustic, cultural, and historical aspects of unfamiliar designs and colors that provide stimulating contrasts to what we know at home. Yet, travel is also an opportunity to look at the modern, minimalist interior decor that is favored in the chic, design-conscious centers of the world—New York, London, Milan, Paris, Tokyo. Traveling out of familiar territory is often the only opportunity we get to see genuinely contemporary furniture or gadgets, and the *crème de la crème* of the latest designs. Immersing yourself in unfamiliar furniture with new shapes, wheels, unexpected colors, and finishes, while in a foreign city, can be remarkably stimulating. You may come home with an uncharacteristic enthusiasm to try something contemporary, or, having experienced a minimalist Italian bathroom, you might want to jettison your claw-foot bath in favor of something sleek, marble and understated.

THE GRAND FINALE

Wanting to decorate with a difference and to go beyond the common melting pot of influences gives added impetus to travel. Most of us know the combination of hassle and satisfaction that you experience as you

haul something like a Turkish rug or stash of rustic china onto the plane, but not everything is so easily transportable. Fortunately, many companies import, adapt, and market most of the inspirational pieces that we come across on our travels. You will almost certainly be able to find hand-loomed Indian cottons, Thai and Indian silks, Provençal tiles in myriad colors, Spanish terra-cottas labs, and African slate. You can buy chunky Greek day beds by mail order, or Indian fretwork furniture, Indonesian painted cupboards, or Mediterranean paint washes. Scour ethnic areas in town for Chinese textiles and lacquered boxes, Indian fabrics, and African baskets. Track down specialist suppliers of a particular style, such as Swedish or Shaker furniture, or maybe Portuguese needle-point rugs. It is worth the search, because one special piece that utterly captures the atmosphere of a far-away place can give the most wonderful grand finale to your scheme.

Opposite When you are abroad, a pile of cobalt-blue tiles, an Indian bench, or hand-woven textiles, seen *in situ* or for sale, may be irresistible. If so, how you interpret and adapt them to your own environment is vital. Perhaps use tiles in smaller quantities, as backsplashes or countertops; or limit bright paint colors to the woodwork. Before an imported element is permanently installed at home, live with it for a while to insure that its transition works and that your enthusiasm for it has survived.

Above Travel provides a feast of extraordinary sights. Interpreting the spirit of a place and allowing its style to influence your decorating may be more interesting than trying to reproduce it in total. In this informal dining room, vivid hues from Greece—hot pink, aqua, lilac, and orange—combine with tiny twinkling lights, a mosaic mirror, and casual country furniture, for a quirky effect that defies definition.

A Memorable Journey

A trip to foreign lands can prompt unique and surprising thoughts. A landscape glimpsed through a train window, the grainy light of a winter's day, or the sun-drenched color in an unfamiliar clime could all provide the stimulus for a new slant on a favorite room. Dignified and serene, this country dining room borrows casually from Sweden's cool Gustavian style. Faux-paneled walls and crisp stripes are played out in gentle tones of tea-rose, white, and chalky gray.

Gathering together the strands of a foreign style is about interpretation, rather than re-creation. Identify classic themes, a dominant mood, and characteristic motifs, shapes, or hues. Then adapt them with a light touch to suit your particular room. The appeal of a Swedish look lies in the mix of the known and unknown, the familiar and the strange. Just one authentic feature—a piece of furniture or an original textile—may form the nucleus of the scheme to come. The investment here is in a good reproduction Swedish dining table and medallion chairs which set the right tone.

A dining room benefits from a poised and formal style which creates the perfect setting for intimate dinners. This low-ceilinged room is rural rather than ornate, and lacks the necessary sophistication to carry off grand furniture. To create a more graceful and elegant space, the walls are painted with *trompe-l'oeil* panels; these give a suggestion of faded grandeur and place the room in an historic context.

Opposite The original sage green walls and chintz draperies were oppressive in this small country room. Pale, airy colors and *trompe-l'oeil* paneling produce a fresher effect.

Above A breathtaking landscape may unleash a new vein of inspiration, as the glint of sun on snow provokes a move toward an unexplored palette.

Left Harking back to a forgotten era of elegance and grace, this peaceful dining room is resplendent with harmonious colors and lovely furniture. It represents the perfect fusion of the best of Gustavian style, with its simple stripes and ornate detailing, combined with a twist of English country prettiness.

Left Identifying a motif characteristic of a certain style is the starting point for soft furnishings. The classic Gustavian two-color pencil stripe is teamed with ticking stripes in varying scales, and a simple Swedish floral. Mixing stripes is infinitely easier when sticking to a rigid color framework. Strawberry, tea-rose, pearly grays, and charcoal form this basic palette.

Below The way that the furniture is arranged in a room is as important as the shapes of the pieces themselves. A single chair against a wall sums up the pared-down style integral to the Gustavian interior.

Opposite When choosing furniture, do not feel too constrained about finding faithful reproductions. Look instead for shapes that feel right and have a similar mood. The curvy cabriole legs, washed gray tones, and simple loop handles of this antique commode mix sympathetically with the reproduction table and chairs. A spacious chest of drawers in a dining room is invaluable, too, for storing table linen, silverware, and candles.

Adapting a look

When traveling abroad, it is often the unfamiliar slant of light that lends a magical air to an otherwise ordinary interior. In hot countries, it is the contrast of light and shade that is novel and exciting, the brilliance of color followed by the bleaching of the sun. More northerly climes shimmer subtly in cool, gray light, so re-creating the shifting nuances of Sweden's soft, diffuse light is a natural starting point for the dining room. A combination of restful grays, from charcoal to chalk, will achieve this and will work with rather than against the lack of light in the room. Pale gray paint is used for the walls, a tone lighter on the ceiling, and a shade darker on the paintwork; two hand-mixed grays outline the faux panels, one with a blue bias and one tending toward brown.

Inspiration for painted faux panels can be found in a quick glance through coffee-table books devoted to Swedish style. Even the grandest Swedish palace used simple paint effects to suggest paneling, and it is a technique that is much easier than it looks. Masking tape provides the only guide you need for keeping the lines straight.

The tonal build-up of grays means that a secondary shade is needed to soften and define the dining room. Faded, soft reds running to pink are classically Swedish. So, too, are striped textiles, which are the staples of the Gustavian look. A pink narrow variety covers the dining chairs, plus a broader stripe to fill the deep window seat, and a bolder cherry-red stripe for a scatter pillow. To break up what could easily become an overabundance of stripes, a delicately drawn Swedish cotton floral is introduced into the scheme.

If you are attempting to reinvent a particular look, you will need to go further than a simple selection of fabrics; it is the way you employ them that is important. Swedish slipcover styles are characteristically relaxed and simply tailored, so tie-on seat covers for the medallion dining chairs are just right. Where an American armchair might sport a box-pleated skirt, here the covers are simple and slightly baggy with the chair legs on full show. You can learn a great deal about slipcovers simply by scrutinizing books or magazines on foreign style or by visiting museums and grand houses. Be prepared to adapt certain elements. Where a Swedish valance may be an understated ruffle of muslin, a more substantial choice is essential here. Two embroidered antique sheets are hung together for curtains and the top is flipped over to create a ruffled effect.

Above A dining room provides myriad opportunities for expanding on pretty motifs and adding new strands. Think of pictorial china for the table, self-patterned linens, etched glasses, and wonderful silverware. Here handblown rustic wine glasses work well with exotically patterned French porcelain because they reflect the mix of styles already forged in the room.

Opposite, below In a pale, color-washed scheme, where pearly grays predominate and the play of light is essential to the look, gentle rather than vivid accent shades are needed. Consider using glass to achieve unusual effects. Tinted wine glasses, glowing against white table linen, are one option here, but so too are glass vases, bowls, or a chandelier tinged with glints of extra color.

Right Adaptation is always essential when reinterpreting a look seen abroad. The way in which a sofa is covered and the manner in which a window is dressed contain vital clues. If a slipcover is a simple, stitched linen affair, then keep your pillows in a similar vein: buttoned, self-paneled, or totally unadorned.

Essential embellishments

When dipping into an unfamiliar style, there are fewer restrictions on what you can and cannot do. In the end, the choices are essentially about what pleases you and what is right for the room. Yet an analysis of a particular style should still be thorough, so you really do achieve the best effect. The enduring appeal of Swedish Gustavian style is its air of elegance tinged with simplicity, so the finishing touches need to reflect this mix. A romantic glass chandelier, a heavily ornate mirror and side table, and ceramics painted with cherries and curlicues all provide the necessary elegance, while plain silver candlesticks, heavy linen napkins, and an unframed oil painting represent the element of restraint. A cluster of strawberry-pink country roses, gathered into an unpretentious glass vase, reflects on a small scale what the entire room achieves.

SUPPLIERS

FABRICS & WALL COVERINGS

Agnes Bourne
2 Henry Adams Street, #220
San Francisco, CA
94103

Ainsworth Noah & Associates
351 Peachtree Hills Avenue
Suite 518
Atlanta, GA
30305

Ashley House
1838 West Broadway
Vancouver, B.C.

Bradbury & Bradbury Wallpapers
940 Tyler Street
Benicia, CA
94510

Calvin Klein Home
654 Madison Avenue
New York, NY
10022

Delk & Morrison, Inc
320 Julia Street
New Orleans, LA
70130

Dream Designs
956 Commercial Drive
Vancouver, B.C.

George Smith
73 Spring Street
New York, NY
10012

Kneedler-Faucher
8687 Melrose Avenue
Los Angeles, CA
90069

Kravet Fabrics Inc.
225 Central Avenue South
Bethpage, NY
11714
www.kravel.com

Norton Blumenthal, Inc.
979 Third Avenue
New York, NY
10022

Patina Finishes and Copper Coats
3486 Kurtz Street, #102
San Diego, CA
92110

Quadrille
D & D Building
979 Third Avenue
New York, NY
10022

Ralph Lauren Home Collection
980 Madison Avenue
New York, NY
10021

Royal Design Studio
386 East H Street
Suite 209-188
Chula Vista, CA
91910

Silk Surplus
235 East 58th Street
New York, NY
10022

Waverly
939 Third Avenue
New York, NY
10022

Valerianne of Vancouver
1445 Bellevue
West Vancouver, B.C.

York Wallcovering and Fabric
201 Carlise
York, PA
17404

FLOORING

ABC Carpet & Home
888 Broadway
New York, NY
10003

Albany Woodworks
PO Box 729
Albany, LA
70711

American Woodmark Corp.
3102 Shawnee Drive
PO Box 1990
Winchester, VA
22601

Ann Sacks Tile and Stone
8120 Northeast 33rd Drive
Portland, OR
97211

Armstrong World Industries
PO Box 3001
Lancaster, PA
17604
www.armstrong.com

Atlas Carpet Mills
2200 Saybrook Avenue
Los Angeles, CA
90040

Axminster Carpets Ltd.
919 3rd Avenue
New York, NY
10022

Azrock Industries
PO Box 3145
Houston, TX
77253

Bomanite Corp
PO Box 599
Madera, CA
93639

Country Floors
15 East 16th Street
New York, NY
10003
or
321 Davenport Road
Toronto, Ontario
M5R 1K5

Daltile
7834 Hawn Freeway
Dallas, TX
75217

Florida Tile Industries Inc.
PO Box 447
Lakeland, FL
33802

Historic Floors of Oshkosh
911 East Main Street
Winneconne, WI
45986

Kentucky Wood Floors
PO Box 33276
Louisville, KY
40232

Nature's Loom
32 East 31st Street
New York, NY
10016

New England Hardwoods
Route 82 South
PO Box 534
Pine Plains, NY
12567

Wilsonart Flooring
2400 Wilson Place
PO Box 6110
Temple, TX
76503-6110

World Mosaic
1665 West 7th Avenue
Vancouver, B.C.

FURNITURE

Aero
132 Spring Street
New York, NY
10012

Belle Epoque Furnishings
1066 Yonge Street
Toronto, Ontario
M4W 2L4

Ethan Allen
2819 N.W. Loop 410
San Antonio, TX

Filamento
2185 Fillmore
San Francisco, CA
94115

FreWil Furniture
605 North La Brea Avenue
Los Angeles, CA
90036

Green Design Furniture
267 Commercial Street
Portland, ME
04101

IKEA
1000 Center Drive
Elizabeth, NJ
stores also located in CA, D.C.,
MD, NY, PA
www.ikea.com

IKEA Canada
Stores located across Canada
including Burlington, Calgary,
Edmonton, and Vancouver
(mail order: 800-661-9807)

Limn
290 Townsend Street
San Francisco, CA
94107

Mike Furniture
2142 Fillmore Street
San Francisco, CA
94115

Mobler Imports Ltd. (Across Canada)
3351 Sweden Way
Richmond, B.C.
or
10550 Mayfield Road
Edmonton, Alberta
T5P 4X4

Norwalk: The Furniture Idea
980 Cambie Street
Vancouver, B.C.
or
1655 United Boulevard
Coquitlam, B.C.

Sauder Woodworking
502 Middle Street
Archbold, OH
43502

Shabby Chic
1013 Montana Avenue
Santa Monica, CA
90403
or
93 Greene Street
New York, NY
10012

Slater Marinoff & Co.
1823 Fourth Street
Berkeley, CA

Seaman's Furniture
300 Crossways Park Drive
Woodbury, NY
11797

Thomasville Furniture Industries
PO Box 339
Thomasville, NC
27361
www.thomasville.com

Zona
97 Greene Street
New York, NY
1001

PAINTS

Crown Berger
Bentley Brothers
2709 South Park Road
Louisville, KY
40219

General Paint
604-253-3131 for stores in
Western Canada
www.generalpaint.com

Glidden Paint Co.
925 Euclid Avenue
Cleveland, OH
44115

Benjamin Moore & Co.
51 Chestnut Ridge Road
Montvale, NJ
07645

Old Fashioned Milk Paint Co.
436 Main Street
PO Box 222
Groton, MA
01450
www.milkpaint.com

Para Paints
(available at paint dealers in the
U.S. and Canada)
800-461-7272

Pittsburgh Paints
1 PPG Place
Pittsburgh, PA
15272

Pratt and Lambert Paints
(available at paint dealers in the
U.S. and Canada)
800-289-7728 for U.S. information
800-364-1359 for Canada
information

Rust-Oleum
11 Hawthorn Parkway
Vernon Hills, IL
60061

Selectone Paints
800-875-9935 for locations in
Canada

Sherwin Williams
101 Prospect Street
Cleveland, OH
44115

INDEX

Page numbers in *italics* refer to photograph captions.

A

accenting
  color 20–1, *22, 23, 27*, 35, 74, 92
  fabric 44–5
  furniture 66
accessories 35, 50, *58, 86, 134*
  bathroom *73, 74*
  bedroom *105, 106*
  home office 121
  in large rooms 112
  See also possessions
apartments 24–9, 57–9
architectural detail *90*, 122–41
art gallery inspiration 79
attics *97*

B

baseboards 126, 127
basements *98*
bathrooms 70–5, *70*, 79, 112, *145*, 148
bedrooms 43, 52–5, *52, 55, 63, 64, 97, 98*, 102–6, *102, 106, 129, 145*
Biedermeier 85, 86, *89*
black and white 70, 75
blues *14, 16*, 22, 23, 35, 52, 55, *57, 81, 83*, 90–2, 98, 99, *110*, 116–21, *121*, 132–4
  aqua *136*, 136–41
bright rooms 97–9
brocades 86

C

candelabra *134, 135*
Caribbean style *136*, 138
carpets 45, *127*, 138, 147

ceramics *78*, 80, 81
  and color *24, 27, 32, 32*, 35, *35, 58*
chairs *16, 20*, 35, 58, *63, 64*, 70, *145, 152*
chandeliers 155
checks *39, 40*, 43, 45, *57*, 58, 134
cinnamon *16*
clutter 83, *115, 134*
color 13–29, 49–50, 90–3
  definition using 127, 128
  exotic 138, *147, 149*
  and fruits *31, 81*
  historical inspiration 17, 19
  in the home office *117*, 120
  in an open plan *110*, 112, 114, 115
  and possessions 79–80
  and stripes *152*
  and sunlight 97–9, *103*
  and vegetables *31*
  See also under names of individual colors: black and white, blues, cinnamon, creams, grays, greens, lavender, lilac, lime, neutrals, ocher, orange, pastel tints, peach, pinks, plum, purples, reds, silver, taupe, whites, yellows
colorboards *32, 58*, 69, *132*
  See also sampleboards
contrast in furniture 66
creams 31, *31, 32, 32*, 35, *35, 58, 97, 129*, 136
curtains and draperies 44, *44*, 45, *58*, 99, 100, 105–6, *132–4, 145*, 147–8
  See also shades; windows
customizing
  fabrics 40, *44*, 106
  furniture 64, 65, *66*, 69, *78*

D

darker rooms 52, *52, 97, 98*, 100–1, 116–17
decay, inspiration from 64, *64*
demarcation of function (in large

spaces) *31, 50, 110*, 114–15
dining rooms 32, *89*, 149, 150–5, *151, 154*
display 35, 83, *83*
doorknobs *138*

E

entry halls and hallways 136–41

F

fabrics 36–59, 144
  bathroom 73, 74, 75
  bedroom 52, 55, *105, 106*
  and color choice 14–17, 23, 27–8, *29, 132*
  design coordinated *105*, 114
  living room 86, *86, 89*
  entry 141
  exotic 147, 148, *149*
  Gustavian (Swedish) 154
  home office 121
  and light 98, 99
  in small rooms 113
fashion as inspiration 17, 85, *85*
fireplaces *90*, 127, 128, 130–5, *130, 131, 134*
floors 27, *40*, 43, 44, 45, 49, 58, 70, 75, *105, 129*, 134
  in darker rooms 100, *101*
  entry hall 136, *136*
  faux tiled 70
  florals *39, 40, 41*, 43, *57, 66*, 75, *89*, 154
  flowers 22, 27, 29, 32, 35, *39*, *5*, 58, 89, 92, *141*, 155
four-poster beds 106, *115*
French style 47–51, *50, 66*, 70, *145*, 148
furniture *11*, 61–75, 148, *152*
  bedroom 55, 106
  entry hall 138
  formal rooms *48, 86*, 89

home office 118
  in large rooms 112, *113*
  and light 100–1
  in small rooms *115*, 118–19

G

glass bricks 100
glassware *50*, 81, *81, 83, 86*, 90–3, *90, 93, 102*, 154
grays *19, 24, 27, 39*, 50, 52, 84–9, *85, 86*, 99, 150–4, *154*
greens *16*, 17, 19, 24–9, *27, 58*, 90–2, 98, 100, 130–5
  aqua *136*, 138
Gustavian look (Swedish) *86*, 118, 126, 150–5

H

hallways and entry halls 136–41
home offices 117–21, *117, 118, 120*

I

ironwork, decorative *124*, 127

K

kitchens 30–5, *31, 64*, 79, 113, 114–15, *115*, 149

L

large rooms *110*, 111–12, *113*
lavender 27, *73*, 86
light 94–107
  and color 22, *29*, 52, *52*

and fabrics 45, 49
  northern 117, 152
  and space 115
lilac *19*, 70–4
lime *75*
linking furniture 66
linking spaces 114
living rooms *40,* 46–51, 85–91, *101,*
  115, 131
lofts *110*

M

maps, hanging 80
Mediterranean style 57, 58, 96
metallic highlights *see* reflective
  surfaces
minimalism 112, 148
mirrors 65, 89, *113,* 135
  See also reflective surfaces
moldings 126–7, 128, *129*
monochrome schemes *22,* 113
motifs for inspiration *39,* 43, 57,
  126, 132, *136,* 141
museum inspiration 79

N

nature, inspiration from 79
neutrals *19, 19,* 21, 28, 30–5, *43,* 85,
  93, 100, *117, 121,* 138, *146*

O

ocher *44*
open-plan areas, defining *31, 50,
  110,* 114–15
orange *14, 19,* 90–2

P

paint
  authentic finishes 128
  charts 14, 22, 128
  distressed 98, 126
  matte *98,* 100, 112, 114
  sample pots 22
paintings. *See under* pictures
paneling 126, *129, 145,* 150, *151,*
  154
pastel tints 20, *20, 31*
pattern 40, *40,* 43, 44–5, *46–51, 55,*
  98, 106
  balancing a Victorian fireplace
    132–4, *132*
  in large spaces 111–12
peach *70*
period style 122–41
pewter *19,* 89
pictures *14, 16,* 28, 78, *78,* 79–81, *81,*
  132, 141, 146
  hanging 83
  in home office *118,* 121
pillows *40, 40, 41, 43, 44, 57,* 86,
  132, 134
  bathroom *74*
  for colour *22, 93*
pinks *14, 16, 19,* 22, *70,* 89, *101,*
  102–7, 149, 150–5, *152*
pitched ceilings *115*
plum 24, *27, 48*
possessions 76–93, 148
purples *23,* 24–9, *47, 47, 48,* 50,
  90–2, *146*

R

radiators 126, 138, *141*
reds *23, 29, 39,* 52–5, *58,* 154
reflective surfaces *97–8,* 100–1, 112,
  138
  metallic highlights *27, 28, 32*
  See also mirrors
restoration costs 128
Roman shades *74,* 120, 134

S

salon style 84–9
sampleboards *10,* 23, *27,* 52, *92*
  See also colorboards
sample pots (paint) 22
satins 49
screens *40,* 115, 145
shades 74, *98,* 99, *101, 101,* 113, 120,
  138, 141
  as partitions 115
  See also curtains and draperies;
    windows
shopping
  abroad 144, 148–9
  for fabrics 38–40, 45, *48*
  for furniture 62, 69
  for traditional materials 128
shutters 28, 99, 105, 126, 148
silver 84–9, *120, 121, 138,* 155
slipcovers *19,* 41, 64, 154, *155*
small rooms 112–21, *113*
space 108–21
spatial enhancement, with matte
  paints 112, 114
stenciling 126
storage 32, 114, 118, *120,* 121, *121*
stripes 22, *39,* 43, 49, *49, 50, 55,* 98,
  111, 114, 120, *152,* 154
studio apartment 24–9
sunlight. *See under* light
swatches
  for color choice 14–17, 22, 23,
    27, 57
  misleading 45
Swedish style *86,* 118, 126, 150–5

T

taupe *19*
textiles *see* fabrics
texture *43, 44,* 45, 49, 55, *86*
  in all-white rooms *98*
  bathroom *73*
  and color 20, 23, 28, 52
  entry hall and hallway 138–40

exotic 147
  in small rooms 113
thematic links (fabrics) 43–4, *62,* 92
tiles 127, 128, 147, *149*
toiles 4, 43, 47, *47,* 48–50, *50,* 52
travel, inspiration from *9,* 143–55
trompe-l'oeil paneling 150, *151*

U

upholstery 41, 45, 49, *66,* 89

V

valances 112, 148, 154
Victorian style 99, 124, 126, 131

W

wallpapers 43, 111, 132, 140, 147
wardrobes *69*
whites 19, *19,* 20, 21, 27, 31, 32, 49,
  52–5, *55,* 120, 150–5
  black and white 70, 75
  white rooms 20, 22, 23, *83, 98,* 99,
    110, 124, *127,* 128
windows 28, *29,* 41, 49, *89, 97,* 101,
  101, 112, 126, 127
  See also curtains and draperies;
    shades

Y

yellows 20, 24–9, 35, *44,* 92, *101,*
  102–7, *102,* 115
  and navy *124*
  perfect 105

ACKNOWLEDGMENTS

AUTHOR ACKNOWLEDGMENTS

I dedicate this book to my husband Anthony, and my children Cicely and baby Felix, whose birth punctuated the writing of this book. With thanks to Denny Hemming, Catriona Woodburn, Rachel Davies, and Alison Fenton at Conran Octopus, for their enthusiasm and tireless hard work on the book. Special thanks, too, to the Homes & Gardens *decorating teams, past and present, for their creative and inspirational transformations.*

PICTURE ACKNOWLEDGMENTS

We would like to thank the following photographers and organizations for their kind permission to reproduce the photographs in this book.

1 Sandra Lane/*Homes & Gardens*/Robert Harding Syndication; 2–3 Polly Wreford/*Homes & Gardens*/Robert Harding Syndication; 4–5 Debi Treloar/*Homes & Gardens*/Robert Harding Syndication; 6 Ben Edwards/Impact; 7 vt wonen; 8 above Jan Baldwin (Cathy O'Clery); 8 below Tony Jones/Robert Harding Picture Library; 9 above Jaques Dirand/The Interior Archive; 9 below Robert Frerck/Robert Harding Picture Library; 10–11 Polly Wreford/*Homes & Gardens*/Robert Harding Syndication; 12–13 Marie-Pierre Morel (Postic, Reyre)/*Marie Claire Maison*; 13 John Miller/Robert Harding Picture Library; 14 Dennis Brandsma/vt wonen; 15 Pascale Chevallier (Michel Klein)/Agence Top; 16 above Trevor Richards/*Homes & Gardens*/Robert Harding Syndication; 16 below Christian Sarramon; 17 vt wonen; 18 Chris Chen/*Belle Magazine*; 19 Frank Brandwijk/vt wonen; 20 Andrew Wood /The Interior Archive (Charles Worthington); 21 Tim Beddow/The Interior Archive; 22 above Habitat UK; 22 below Andrew Wood/The Interior Archive; 23 David Churchill/ Arcaid(Stickland Coombe Architects); 24–29 Tom Leighton/*Homes & Gardens*/Robert Harding Syndication; 30–35 Debi Treloar/*Homes & Gardens*/ Robert Harding Syndication; 36–37 Jan Baldwin (Cathy O'Clery); 37 Adam Woolfitt/Robert Harding Picture Library; 38 Simon Brown/The Interior Archive; 39 above David Phelps; 39 below Richard Holt/*Homes & Gardens*/ Robert Harding Syndication; 40 James Merrell/*Homes & Gardens*/Robert Harding Syndication; 41 Solvi Dos Santos; 42 Rodney Weidland/*Vogue Living*; 43 left Henry Wilson/The Interior Archive; 43 right Hotze Eisma; 44 vt wonen; 45 Ray Main; 46–51 Pia Tryde/*Homes & Gardens*/Robert Harding Syndication; 52–55 Polly Wreford/*Homes & Gardens*/Robert Harding Syndication; 56–59 Debi Treloar/*Homes & Gardens*/Robert Harding Syndication; 60–61 Polly Wreford/*Homes & Gardens*/Robert Harding Syndication; 61 right Simon Kenny/*Vogue Living*; 62 Hotze Eisma; 63 Marie-Pierre Morel (Paula Navone, D. Rosensztroch); 64 Marie-Pierre Morel (D. Rosensztroch)/*Marie Claire Maison*; 65 vt wonen; 66 Solvi Dos Santos; 67 Tim Goffe/The Interior Archive; 68 Andreas von Einsiedel/ *Homes & Gardens*/Robert Harding Syndication; 69 Hotze Eisma; 70–75 Debi Treloar/ *Homes & Gardens*/Robert Harding Syndication; 76–77 Ray Main (Gottelier Home; Designers of Artwork Knitwear); 77 Patricia Aithie/Ffotograff; 78–79 Tim Beddow/The Interior Archive; 78 Solvi Dos Santos; 80 left Simon Upton/ The Interior Archive; 81 David Parmiter/ *Homes & Gardens*/Robert Harding Syndication; 82 Marie-Pierre Morel (Sty. C. Ardouin)/*Marie Claire Maison*; 83 Jan Baldwin (Cathy O'Clery); 84–89 Debi Treloar/*Homes & Gardens*/Robert Harding Syndication; 90–93 Debbie Patterson/*Homes & Gardens*/Robert Harding Syndication; 94 Simon Upton/ World of Interiors; 95 Simon Brown/The Interior Archive; 96–97 Paul Ryan/International Interiors (Designer: Laura Bohn); 97 Fritz von der Schulenburg/ The Interior Archive; 98 Andrew Wood/The Interior Archive (Charles Worthington); 99 Nicolas Tosi (C. Ardouin)/*Marie Claire Maison*; 100 Christian Sarramon; 101 Otto Polman/Ariadne; 102–107 Polly Wreford/ *Homes & Gardens*/Robert Harding Syndication; 108 Simon Brown/The Interior Archive; 109 Jason Hawkes Aerial Collection/Julian Cotton Photo library; 110 Ray Main; 111 Hotze Eisma; 112 Andrew Wood/The Interior Archive; 113 Gilles de Chabaneix (sty. Marie Kalt)/*Marie Claire Maison*; 114 Marie-Pierre Morel (D. Rozenzstroch); 115 above Jan Verlinde (Pieter Vandenhout); 115 below Alexander van Berge; 116–121 Polly Wreford/*Homes & Gardens*/Robert Harding Syndication; 122 vt wonen; 123 Pascale Chevalier/ Agence Top (Nicole & Pierre de Fayet); 124 Andrew Wood/The Interior Archive; 125 Mads Mogensen; 126 Fritz von der Schulenburg/The Interior Archive; 127 vt wonen; 128 Simon Brown/The Interior Archive; 129 above Marie-Pierre Morel (Postic/ Reyre)/ *Marie Claire Maison*; 129 below Ariadne; 130–135 Debi Treloar/*Homes & Gardens*/Robert Harding Syndication; 136–141 Tom Leighton/*Homes & Gardens*/Robert Harding Syndication; 142 Marie-Pierre Morel (Sty: Christine Peuch)/*Marie Claire Maison*; 143 The Image Bank; 144 above Marie-Pierre Morel(Stylist: C. Ardouin)/*Marie Claire Maison*; 144 below Lucinda Symons; 145 Simon Upton/ World of Interiors; 146 William Waldron (Sherrie Donghia); 147 Ray Main; 148–149 Henry Wilson/The Interior Archive; 150–155 Debi Treloar/*Homes & Gardens*/Robert Harding Syndication.